Evolutio

"In *Evolutionary Love Relationships*, Andrew Harvey and Chris Saade have revealed the love we have always dreamed of. Their gorgeous book is a radiant call to evolutionary love: where sex can be holy, orgasm a conduit to the divine, and intimate love, the expansion of justice, peace, unity on this earth. It made me want to love again."
— EVE ENSLER, Activist and Author of *The Vagina Monologues* and *In the Body of the World*

"This is a daring book, a needed one and a timely one. It challenges the idolatry of sentimental and privatized love, yes of narcissistic love, that the modern age has bequeathed to us. It carries us into a new paradigm of relationships that integrates both the beauty and the suffering, the ecstasy and the anguish, of the world. It puts all efforts at human love—from friendship to creativity to forgiveness to love making—into the greater context of a sacred and evolving cosmic history and with it the responsibility of divinizing culture so that healing, celebrating and justice-making are nurtured and sustained. This book enlightens the heart and challenges the comfortable to awaken a single and sacred fire expressed in both the compassion of intimacy and the compassion of service that the world is hungry for."
— MATTHEW FOX, Author & Religious Scholar

"Every age has its teachers, who keep the eternal truths alive for all of us. And when a generation is very, very lucky, it encounters a teacher so illumined that the words he delivers must be illumined as well. In the case of Andrew Harvey, the light he sheds is like a meteor burst across the inner sky."

—MARIANNE WILLIAMSON, Spiritual Teacher, Author & Lecturer

"What would the world look like if two people, deeply in love with each other, harnessed the energy of their connection for the benefit of all beings and the Earth Herself? In this exciting new book, sacred activists Andrew Harvey and Chris Saade draw on a lifetime of passionately engaged spiritual practice to lift up a vision of intimate relationship as a holy fire to dissolve and transform the most intractable social and environmental crises."

—MIRABAI STARR, Author of *Caravan of No Despair*

"The direct experience of love—honest, ragged, roll up your sleeves and get in the mud kind of love—is needed now more than ever in the world. In this book, Harvey and Saade show readers how to live from this place of authentic and unconditional love in a way that can quite literally change the world. Please, read this book and see for yourself."

—CHRIS GROSSO, Author of *Indie Spiritualist* and *Everything Mind*

"A sizzling collaboration unfettered by the canards of self-absorbed, new age spirituality interested only in personal happiness. Andrew and Chris dare to encourage a full engagement in sacred activism, sacred sexuality, a celebration of diversity and many more of the deeper understandings while never failing to "honor the paradox of joy and grief." Keep this book near at hand if ever your canvas of life starts to pale."

—CATHERINE INGRAM, Author of *In the Footsteps of Gandhi, Passionate Presence,* and *A Crack in Everything*

"This is a powerful and innovative roadmap that outlines the essential evolution of human relationships. Its practical advice is coupled with revolutionary concepts that wholly redefine and elevate what it means to love in today's modern world. Far beyond what others have even attempted, these words will be referenced for decades to come."

—SCOTT BLUM, Co-founder, *DailyOM*

"We're living in a world that is making less and less sense. Our world needs healing. We need tools that can help us mobilize what's best in our souls and work for a world that shines with possibility, compassion and justice. This book is such a tool. Read this, and your heart will be changed. Pray this, and it will enable you to find depth in human relationships that you didn't know was possible. Act on it, and it will help you dedicate your life to working for a world your heart knows is possible. It's time to stop playing small and settling for half-truths. What we need is a spiritual revolution. May these two wise teachers, through what they share in this book, take your hand and guide you into the center of your heart and empower you to live from there. The future of the world depends on it."

—ADAM BUCKO, co-author of *Occupy Spirituality*

"Love is more than a river of warm flowing sentiments and emotion; love is living, evolving, and in action. And the world is urgently crying out for empowered couples to expand their devotion beyond its borders by answering love's highest calling to be of service. Love is alive and in action when two hearts join to become compassionately engaged with humanity's spiritual and material needs alike, and to allow their shared passion to break the banks and meet the necessities of our cherished earth. This book will inspire and instruct bonded pairs in any station of life to step closer to one another as they hearken to love's earnest call to preserve our planet and serve in tandem on every level."

—SUSAN FRYBORT, author of *Hope is a Traveler*, and *Open Passages*

"Here is a vision of partnership, a vision of love itself, that cracks open the cramped confines of expectation and disappointment that can plague a relationship, and widens the heart into the companionship of the Divine. *Evolutionary Love Relationships* shows us the greatest gift of coupledom—that by devoting yourselves together in service to what lies beyond your private love, you deepen into the true source of love, and into the true passion of your life. This beautiful book will help move the whole world forward."

—PHILIP SHEPHERD, author of *New Self New World*

"Nearly twenty years ago my beloved husband, Brian Hilliard, taught me: In basic arithmetic, one plus one equals two but in Soulmate Math, one plus one equals eleven and your love blesses and heals the world. If you are ready to blow your heart open, embrace and exude your passion, and elevate your love to serve the world, then I highly suggest you use this book as your guide. Now, more than ever, the world needs your love."

—ARIELLE FORD, author of *Turn your Mate into your Soulmate*

Evolutionary
Love Relationships
Passion, Authenticity, and Activism

Andrew Harvey & Chris Saade

ENREALMENT PRESS,
TORONTO, CANADA

Published by Enrealment Press
PO Box 64
Acton, Ontario
Canada L7J 2M2

Cover design by Susan Frybort
Book design by Allyson Woodrooffe (go-word.com)
Printed in the USA

Library and Archives Canada Cataloguing in Publication

Harvey, Andrew, 1952-, author
      Evolutionary love relationships: passion, authenticity
& activism / Andrew Harvey and Chris Saade.

Includes bibliographical references. Issued in print and electronic formats.
ISBN 978-0-9947843-3-9 (paperback). --ISBN 978-0-9947843-4-6 (pdf)

      1. Religion and social problems. 2. Spiritual life. 3. Couples.
4. Environmentalism. I. Saade, Chris, author II. Title.

BL65.S64H37 2016   201'.77   C2016-905000-9
                                                   C2016-905001-7

Dedications

Andrew Harvey

To Howard and Sheryl with all love and gratitude.

Chris Saade

This book is dedicated to all those who are seeking to build partnerships based on the freedom of authenticity and the passion of global solidarity. Your path is noble in its hopes, struggles, defeats and breakthroughs.

Contents

Acknowledgements   xi

Foreword by Jeff Brown   xvii

Introduction (Andrew)   xxiii

Introduction (Chris)   xxvii

Section 1
Evolutionary Love

Chapter 1   The Vision of Love   2

Chapter 2   Passion   37

Section 2
The Six Keys of Heart-Centered Living and Evolutionary Relationship Building

Chapter 3   Honor Individual Authenticity   70

Chapter 4   Honor the Paradox of Joy and Grief   88

Chapter 5   Honor the Heart   108

Chapter 6   Advocate Idiosyncratic Differences   127

Chapter 7   Co-Create a Vision of Solidarity   143

Chapter 8   Celebrate   160

Section 3
Eros and Evolutionary Sexuality

Chapter 9   Delving into the Fullness of Sacred Sexuality   184

Chapter 10   Pursuing Evolutionary Love   214

About the Authors   224

Acknowledgements

—Andrew Harvey

To Janet Thomas, for her unerring eye.
To Jenny Di Angelo, for her passion and help.
To Jeff Brown, for believing.
To Anne Andrews, for her staunchness.
To Frances and Mike Calhoun, whose love inspires me.
To Ellen Gunter, great friend and co-conspirator.
To Jill Angelo, soul-sister and true sacred activist.
To Caroline Myss, always.

Acknowledgements
—Chris Saade

My ability to participate in the creation of this book is largely due to the support, love, input, feedback, challenges, partnerships, and life-lessons afforded me by precious relationships. A quick mention here will only portray a tiny bubble of my gratitude.

First, to my wife, Jessie Thompson, I offer my deepest gratitude for her spirit. I am blessed by her commitment to look outward with me in service to the world. She is a passionate advocate for diversity, justice, and inclusion. I am gifted by her loving support.

To my daughter, Amal Maria, I cannot thank her enough for her insightful wisdom, and for her inspiration as she contributes to the community through her dramatic artistry, among them her efforts to serve children and promote causes of justice. I am very grateful for her beautiful heart and spirit. I am also very grateful to my wonderful stepsons, their partners, and my son-in-law.

To Andrew Harvey, the co-creator of this book and my dear friend, I offer plenty of heartfelt thanks. I honor his sacred pursuit of the relationships of the future. His work calls me to my edge and inspires me to go for broke. I am grateful for the dance we do, inspiring one another to greater heights within our work and our pursuit of love-in-action for the Earth, its people, and animals. He is undoubtedly a most generous and passionate heart fire.

In addition to my family, I am blessed by many companions of heart and soul. To Casey Robertson, my soul sister, I celebrate the deep diving she does in her life to live authentically, and the rich nuggets of wisdom she mines from her unremitting pursuit of authenticity and generously brings to our dialogues. Her huge heart, nurturing, and intuitive nature fuel and feed my pioneering work. I also want to thank Barry Sherman for our cherished decades of friendship, his years of service to children, championing the disadvantaged, and speaking truth to power. He is ever present to me in my writings. To Ginger Wagoner, my long standing friend, I offer much gratitude for her genuine heart-dedication to the work we do. In addition to being an artist and highly skilled photographer, she is also my trusted assistant, an excellent editor, and a voice for justice and diversity.

The choice to write has brought me the gift of working with many other people of soul and great commitment. I commend Victoria Gailey, our fantastically detailed office manager, for her thoroughness, creative problem solving, and commitment to the message I endeavor to promote. To Sarah Mae Baucom, I offer great appreciation for her excellent assistance. Her good nature and wise mind is an enrichment to our time working together. Likewise, I am grateful to stellar editors Janet Thomas, Jenny D'Angelo, and Jessica Bowling.

Their commitment to refining my voice and yet keeping it true to my spirit is a talent in itself, as well as their commitment to detail and prompt assistance.

My sincere appreciation for our publisher Jeff Brown is profound. To Jeff, I offer my gratitude for his passion, his care for a heartfelt relatedness with others, and his desire to advance a deeper way of loving for humanity. I am thrilled by our common interest in pursuing a spirituality of the self, one that refuses self-bashing and self-transcendence, and instead hungers to see each self matured into nobility and service.

I also wish to extend my gratitude to my dearest friends of the heart, my companions of the self and spiritual development circles at the Institute for Life-Leadership and Coaching (theilc.org) and at the Olive Branch Center (theolivebranchcenter.net). I am indebted to them for the countless weekend retreats of exploration, delving deep into the heart, cultivating cutting-edge relationship tools, and, mostly, supporting one another's raw authenticity. Their wit, intellect, commitment to authenticity, joie de vivre, and pursuit of love-in-action have all contributed greatly to my journey as a writer.

And to those of you inspired to pick up this book and discover its contents for yourselves, I am grateful that there are people like you in the world. Thank you for joining us in our pursuit of evolutionary love relationships.

Foreword

At a time when a plethora of ungrounded and dissociative spiritual perspectives are taking flight in the west, it is profoundly important that we craft and root models of an embodied and relational nature to bring us back into balance. For far too long, spirituality has been framed as an isolationist, vertical experience, bereft of feeling and unconcerned with its impact on the external world. You find something called "enlightenment" alone on the meditation cushion, while floating through the fragrant emptiness, in the transcending of your physical form, personal identity, "pain body," life story and ego. A funny kind of unity consciousness, where everything that challenges us on Mother Earth is removed from the non-dual field, and where we attempt to access unity in solitude, independent of our fellow humans. While I appreciate that detaching from the world is sometimes necessary, I also appreciate that detachment is a tool, it's not a life. We can only do so much to heal and transform this planet from up high. The real work happens in the trenches of relatedness, with our feet planted firmly on the ground. When we forget this, when we confuse self-avoidance with enlightenment, our spiritual practices begin to look remarkably similar to the economic practices of the unconscionably capitalistic—where the narcissistic quest for mastery and individual achievement comes at the expense of the environment and the world around us. We imagine ourselves actualized or enlightened, while ignoring the plight of those less fortunate and doing nothing to better humankind.

When *Evolutionary Love Relationships* came across my publisher's desk at Enrealment Press, I breathed a deep sigh of relief. It not only reflects the grounded and inclusive framework that I wish to publish, it takes the perspective that I have written from to the next level. In my book, *An Uncommon Bond*, I acknowledged the ability of certain love relationships to somehow crack the karmic code, catapulting each lover into a vaster and more expansive consciousness, one far more vital and inclusive than anything they could experience alone. In other words, I championed the idea that our most expanded spiritual path may actually arise relationally, in the heart of our connections. At the same time, I acknowledged that sustaining these glimpses into eternity is no easy feat. It requires an ongoing and determined willingness to work through everything that comes up to obstruct and undermine the connection. It requires a deep regard for each other's authenticity. It requires a commitment to the relationship itself, as spiritual practice.

Chris Saade and Andrew Harvey invite us to the next stage of relatedness in *Evolutionary Love Relationships*. They remind awakening couples to also turn their energy outward, converting the sacred fire at the heart of their connection into a bonfire of giving that transforms the world we live in. There was a time when I believed that such couples had to shield themselves from the world until they had worked through their issues, but this was too narrow a perspective. It didn't allow the couple to bring their vital energy into the world where it is needed and, as importantly, it didn't invite them to be healed and influenced and deepened and humanized and elevated by the world, itself. Why can't conscious unions touch some of their depths while staring into each other's eyes, and some of it, while staring into the eyes of humanity? Why can't we take action to work through our personal issues, while simultaneously taking action to work through our collective challenges? At this undeniably difficult stage of human development, I am not sure it can happen any other way.

One of the many things I love about this book is that its invitation to sacred activism is not only restricted to intimate relationships. It's an inclusive invitation that also extends to other significant pairings in our lives: like-minded business colleagues, passionate friendships, and benevolent revolutionaries with a shared vision. We see a reflection of this in the book itself, where Andrew and Chris co-create and clarify their perspective through heartfelt dialogue. In addition, this book does not limit its message to those love connections that are psycho-therapeutically focused or spiritually oriented. The call to sacred activism is equally available to those couples who have no interest in such matters, but who are interested in bringing their energy into the world to effect change. And for those conflictual couples who find themselves trapped inside of a tumultuous tomb of trauma, triggers and transference, this book's call to action may well bring their connection back into the light. There may be no better way to remember what we loved about each other, than seeing one another give love to the world.

The book's message is equally as inclusive with respect to the ways we choose to take action. Although the authors discuss activism in heightened and sacred terms, what they are describing is entirely attainable and down-to-earth, even for those who are overwhelmed in their daily life. Make no mistake, this is not a rarefied path only available to the few couples who have the time and money to walk it. A pairing does not have to devote their entire life to a sacred cause in order to reflect the principles at the heart of this book. It can be as simple, and as profound, as spotting a disenfranchised neighborhood kid and offering him work around your home, making lunches and hand delivering them to the homeless, devoting one day a month to cleaning up the river banks near your home. Anything that reflects your authentic nature, and simultaneously heals and elevates the world we live in. Stand on any street corner near you and look around with your eye of compassion and you will see endless opportunities for sacred activism. Your help is needed everywhere. If you think of all the energy that lives at the heart of powerful pairings and couples, you can easily imagine how much world change is possible if some of that energy is loved forward to those who need it. A cosmic and earthly win-win. The kind of gifts that keep on giving.

The important thing is that we do something. Painting a vision of ultimate possibility is a wonderful thing, but only if we are willing to do the real-time work to make it possible. It's fine to point out what is wrong with a system, but far finer to couple that criticism with efforts to change it. If All-oneness means anything, it means that we actually get into the trenches together and take steps to co-create a world of divine possibility. That is what this profound book is inviting—a revolution of efforted connectiveness, one that celebrates accomplishment as a relational construct, with mutual benefit as our shared goal. Our rocket ship takes flight only when everyone gets a seat, and if we reach that stage, we may well stop looking up to the skies for our liberation. We may find it right down here, on the bridge between our hearts.

As this sacred text demonstrates, we are not just here together to keep each other company. We are here together to show each other God. The portal is each other. And that portal opens when we share our hearts—and our most benevolent, devotional intentions—with each other. Sacred activism is not simply a way to heal and transform the material world. It's a way we become God together. Every act of giving and receiving is an act of divine co-creation. With this in mind, it is my prayer that you receive Andrew and Chris's offering in the way that it is intended—as an act of sacred generosity that inspires you to love our world forward. From one giving heart to another...

—JEFF BROWN, Toronto, Canada

Introduction
—Andrew Harvey

Eight years ago now, I received a telephone call from Chris Saade inviting me to Charlotte, to open the Olive Branch Center he had co-created with his wife, Jessie Thompson. I went to Charlotte, baptized the center with a wild speech on Rumi, and found in Chris and Jessie two of the greatest friends of my life. Here were two extraordinary people, united in deep respect for each other and dedicating their lives and resources to fostering a vision of universal love in action beyond the confines of religious dogma, and doing so with rare humility and even rarer passion. I was deeply moved not only by them, but by those I met who had been Chris's pupils for a long time, each of whom in their own unique way, had risen exhilaratingly to Chris's challenge to claim their own authentic self and enact its sacred mission in the world.

In Chris Saade, I met a lion of a man, brilliant, learned in many disciplines, formidably articulate, and committed with a burning and focused intensity to shaping and inspiring a hope-charged vision for a new humanity that resonated on every level with my own. We immediately "recognized" each other; Chris and I are both outsiders in the American spiritual world: I am English and Chris is Lebanese; we both are aghast at New Age superficiality and narcissism; and we both derive our deepest inspiration from the great mystics and poets and the pioneering iconoclastic philosophers of the European tradition, especially Nietzsche, whose brilliance of style and forensic acuteness of intellect continue to galvanize us.

In the following years, Chris and I created together an academy for sacred leadership, taught together often, which only increased my admiration for the radical clarity of Chris's vision, and whenever we met, talked long and passionately into the night about the world crisis we are in and the potential solutions to it. It became increasingly clear to me that Chris is one of our most authentic, inspired and challenging contemporary teachers.

I was honored to introduce, in the sacred activism series I co-edit for North Atlantic Books, Chris's magnificent book, Second Wave Spirituality, and two other books of his gorgeous electric prayers for solidarity, inclusiveness and justice, five of which I included in my anthology of prayers for Hay House, Light the Flame. Few things give me greater joy than to use whatever position I may have to make available to others the voices and testamonies of those I admire. I don't just admire what Chris has achieved and who he is; I continue to learn both from his work and from him, especially from his relentless and clear-eyed commitment to an epic vision of human evolution and to the rugged joy that infuses it on every level. There have been many times when Chris's ability to take the long view has inspired and steadied me and even more occasions when his wise and brotherly critiques of imbalances in my own presentation of my vision have helped me forge a more mature and grounded style, both in the way I speak and teach and in the vision I offer. My gratitude for what he has given me and continues to give me is profound and boundless.

I am especially delighted to introduce our collaborative dialogues on "Evolutionary Love Relationships." Until I met Chris, I had not encountered anyone who believed, as fervently as I do, in the necessity of a radical new vision of love and sexuality and personal relationships to inform and transform our world. Chris and I both honor Rimbaud's great challenge in Les Illuminations; "Il Faut Etre Absolutement Moderne. Il Faut Reinventer L'Amour". "We must be absolutely modern. We must reinvent love." We both know that the privatization of relationships fosters exaggerated projections and a deadening narcissism in a world already enslaved to inauthenticity on every level. Even more importantly, we both know from our lived experience that a sacred relationship is the essential fuel for sustaining and inspiring sacred action in the world.

May these dialogues that were initiated in Charlotte four years ago excite and encourage us all to go deeper into the fire of the Love that longs to initiate us all into its all-transforming power and selfless passion to serve all beings in the life of the creation!

As Rumi wrote:

Mount the stallion of love and do not fear the path;
Love's stallion knows the way exactly
However black with obstacles the path may be.

Introduction

—Chris Saade

Every act of compassion, every moment of kindness, and every single touch of tenderness are jewels of our humanity. We are pioneers excavating the consciousness of love. And what could be more valuable than the giving and receiving of genuine love—the love that flows from our trembling hearts, from our burning chests to the heart of others; a love that is the memory of the eternal.

Love is not a sacrificing of the integrity of our spirit. Love is a generous giving, from a well-nurtured heart, to those who are hungry to receive. If we abandon our spirit, if we betray our authenticity, we lose our passion to love. The heart needs freedom to expand into love.

I want to share some thoughts with you that are important for this exploration of evolutionary love and evolutionary relationships—an exploration that I am so honored to do with Andrew Harvey, a true pioneer of the heart and the spirit, and a man who inspires myriads to love at the edge of love! I desire to say more about the delight of working with my dear friend Andrew—a great pleasure of soul, but first, I want to underline the amazingly potent and promising ideas of evolutionary love and evolutionary relationships. These ideas allow us to envision an empowered and passionate relationship beyond the endless power conflicts and the routine doldrums to which we have been accustomed. They invite us to imagine what love can be: generous, flowing, expressive, and solid. Such love, when passionately offered and passionately received, renews our energy and revitalizes our sense of purpose. It is the love that flows from the unmitigated freedom of authenticity as well as from the pursuit of active solidarity. We can clearly affirm now, that the psychology and the spirituality of *authenticity* and *solidarity* are crucial for our times— authenticity unfolding into solidarity, and solidarity emerging from our particular authentic calling!

The world direly needs couples in love with each other and in love with the Earth, hand in hand acting for causes of peace, solidarity, and the heart. Through my own journey, my relationship pain, and witnessing the pain of others and the world, I have come to know at a cellular level how much a leap forward in our idea of relationship is needed. I have also learned through this journey how much joy is tied to the necessary freedom to be who we are, to generously support our partner in their authenticity, and to practice socially engaged love with our partner!

The coming together of these two seminal concepts—*individual authenticity* and *active solidarity*— unlocks the door for a historical evolutionary leap. It is only when we come to grasp the breadth and depth of the meaning of authenticity, that we will begin to understand the dynamics that initiate a healthy and sustainable loving relationship. The same should be said about grasping the crucial importance of solidarity—and thus the activism of love—and its great contribution to the flowering of individuals and couples. We cannot say enough about how the coming together of the ideas of passionate authenticity (freedom) and profound solidarity (love-in-action) are revolutionizing our thinking and opening up an evolutionary vista for the unfolding of love. It is the unfolding of a new horizon for the intimacy of hearts—a horizon of immense magnitude for bonding, pleasure, and strength. It is true that we are a generation facing harrowing and most dangerous challenges, but we are also the recipients of a most fascinating leap in intelligence.

Although this book focuses on evolutionary love as applied primarily to romantic relationships, whether straight or gay, please know that the principles we are discussing apply to all relationships: romantic couples, intimate family connections, friendships, and even advanced professional partnerships. Each relationship is tremendously important and can be enriched and empowered by founding itself on authenticity and active solidarity.

Nowadays, long term relationships (including marital) are experiencing a tragic sense of paralysis. The psychological myth of our century is that we "must change." That myth has failed us. We are led to believe that we can fundamentally change who we are and change our partners, or at least lead them to the psychotherapist's office where they will supposedly change. This myth is a secular version of an old religious mythology—that of redemption. The priests heralding change (or the unintentional psychotherapists) will, in their "great wisdom," help us make that change if we accept their authority. That way of thinking implies an original flaw in our being/personality and a blatant disregard for the strong roots of authenticity, be it genetic or archetypal authenticity. On a practical level, that belief system has led mainly to decades of debacles in couples' counseling. Allow me to pause here for a moment to clarify a crucial point. I have spent many years as a psychotherapist and I believe in the power of psychotherapy. However, there is a very important distinction I want to draw between psychotherapies that value and respect authenticity and help people move forward by integrating their authenticity (of personality, desires, and preferences), versus those that neglect authenticity and base everything on past causality. Family of origin work is very important and will color how we think about our life and others. However, the purpose of family of origin work is to help reclaim the authentic aspects of ourselves that were denied or repressed, not to question who we are and make it contingent on past events. The new axiom in our thinking is that authenticity is part of the bedrock of life. We know now through archetypal work and especially genetic exploration that individuals have a given structure of authenticity that is part of their truth of being, not something that was caused and thus can be altered. There is a lot in our approach to life that psychotherapy can help us question, clean up, and mature. But the basic authentic nature of individuals cannot be changed and no one should seek to engineer it. To the contrary, the authenticity of our self needs to be profoundly respected.

The greatest problem for individuals (and everyone in a relationship) is that depression results from the denial or the repression of authenticity. We need to choose to ennoble the expression of our authenticity, but we cannot reconstruct our fundamental nature. The integrity of authentic personalities, in their large array of diversity, has to be respected. An approach which is respectful of authenticity affirms individual specificity and calls for a solid partnership that respects freedom as well as a partnership that jointly pursues causes of solidarity and social justice. Such an approach does not ask for change in our authentic nature. Rather, it encourages a conscious and intentional decision to develop one's authenticity into a full-bodied expression of love. It is neither our nature nor our authenticity that is changed or needs to be changed. Actually, the flowering of love comes from a deep and mutual respect of authenticity as well as our inherent connection with global solidarity.

The approach of individual authenticity and global solidarity reflects the foundational principles of democracy in our daily lives: utmost importance of freedom, partnerships based on freedom, respect of diversity, and the necessity of engaged citizenship. In many ways what we are looking for is an internalization of democratic principles into couples' work. Suffice it to say here how important democracy is—both at a collective as well as a couple's level—and how important it is to value and protect our democracies. This statement is very poignant especially today as we are finding our democratic ideals dangerously besieged by too many financial, religious, spiritual, and secular leaders who do not comprehend the evolutionary and most crucial importance of democratic practices.

I am so excited that Andrew and I have partnered in writing this book. He is a very dear friend of my heart, an amazing soul, and an amazing spirit. His passion for life is and has been a glowing ember of inspiration in my heart's fire. He is a man who has dedicated his life to travel all over the world—from Australia, to France, to England, to North America, to Africa—to spread the message of the sacred activism of love, to speak to people about awakening to love-in-action, and engaging in transformative endeavors for social justice and ecological sustainability. And he does so from his heart and from a place of deep spirituality. His staunch insistence on the sacred activism of love has influenced a whole generation of spiritual seekers and helped redirect the spiritual discourse toward a serious, most needed, and socially and ecologically caring sense of love-in-action. It is a treat and privilege to be with Andrew Harvey in this exploration of the evolution of our understanding of love. Andrew's heart and mind are astounding rivers and sacred epic mountains. So is his unceasing passion for empowered, liberated, and divinely rooted individuals. This conversation between Andrew and myself will lead us, and the readers, to reflect deeply on what empowers love and relationships; and do so from a psychological and a spiritual perspective, and from the confluence of these two disciplines.

I also want to say that as we explore the steps of this vision of evolutionary relationships, it is very important to remember that the ideas we are delving into *are not* and *should not* become heavy expectations against which we judge our current relationships. This is extremely important. We do not want to create a check-off list and use it to judge ourselves, our partner, or our relationships. This exploration is like a guiding star of evolution, one that we are all tending toward. We must remember that we are evolving and that evolution is a slow and very emanating process. Every small step we take to move forward will enrich our relationship, empower it, and make it more fulfilling. We are all growing into these possibilities. None is fully there yet. However, when love emerges from an affirmation of individual authenticity and a practice of global solidarity, we know that every exchange is a moment of exquisite and unforgettable beauty (and celebration of life). Once again, do not judge your current relationship by these ideals. Let them be a guiding star for you to significantly enrich your relationship.

As we begin, I want to share with you something that Saint-Exupery, famous for his book The Little Prince, expressed. He states it most succinctly in Wind, Sand and Stars: "Life has taught us that love does not consist in gazing at each other but in looking outward together in the same direction." In other words, a relationship is about looking together toward the great vision that pulls us forward. Saint-Exupery's message was prophetic. He shared it at a time when we were not yet fully grasping the meaning and the richness of what it is to have a relationship that is oriented towards serving the world from a place of strong individual authenticity. A relationship that thrives amid our respect for authenticity, yet is also joined, united, energized, and catalyzed by a common vision of service, of love-in-action. In this exploration of evolutionary relationships, we will travel with you step-by-step as we explore the psychological and spiritual principles of evolutionary, energized, and inspired relationships.

After we speak of love and passion, we will follow the outline of the model of Integra ©, a model of heart-centered living that I have developed after decades of work as a psychotherapist, coach, and teacher of hundreds of psychological development retreats. The model of Integra was born out of the desire to bring together the freedom of individual authenticity with the crucial importance of the pursuit of solidarity, peace, and social justice. I found that the merging of these two seminal tenets is most evolutionary, and propels our consciousness light years forward.

This is the outline for the six steps of the Integra model:

INTEGRA MODEL

The Six Keys of Heart-Centered Living and Leadership
*~A Path to the Freedom of Individual Authenticity
and Global Solidarity~*

I.
Honor and champion the authentic nature of your
unique self and the authentic nature of the
unique self of others.

II.
Honor and champion the paradoxes of joy and grief,
success and defeats, gain and loss.

III.
Honor and champion the deepest desires of your heart
and the deepest desires of the heart of others.

IV.
Honor and champion others in their idiosyncratic
spirit and advocate their differences.

V.
Co-create an inclusive vision of peace and justice with
others that joins your essence with theirs.

VI.
Passionately celebrate the process of co-creation and
the journey toward authenticity and solidarity.

Section 1

Evolutionary Love

Chapter 1
The Vision of Love

Love
—Chris Saade

At this moment in time, when our civilization is being challenged at its roots, a new vision of relationship is arising out of the dire needs of our planet. This new kind of relationship is based on partnerships united by a vision of loving service out in the world. The old paradigm saw partners retreating into one another, which led to a catastrophe in relationship building.

The statistics are horrifying. More than fifty percent of marriages end in divorce and of the other fifty percent, many, if not most, end up in dead relationships. Relationships cannot be enclosed into themselves. In this new evolutionary vision, individuals find the energy of their partnership love through a fierce fidelity to their individual authenticity as well as a passionate and engaged service of the world. They are joined together, out of the truth of their authenticity, in a vision of building justice, peace, democratic freedoms, solidarity, and compassion.

Love is an evolutionary soul force. It is the most powerful force of evolution that we know in our species and in the Universe. Love itself is evolving. The idea of love is evolving in our consciousness. Love is becoming more and more of a central philosophy that defines the fullness of life. Love is becoming something that colors our whole life.

Love helps us understand how we work, how we relate to others in society, and, of course, love propels us into a thriving and unique relationship with our loved one, and with our children. We are also coming to understand that love is a participation with the world in its collective struggle. The form of that participation will differ according to the diversity in our personality and gifts. Love is that which fuels our vitality. Frequently, it is love that fuels the struggle we undertake to survive dire poverty, the struggle to survive ecological problems, the struggle to survive the forces that are fighting against democracy, and the struggle to create a world that really works and offers us a sense of solidarity with one another. Love is the foundation.

Love is also one and indivisible. A lot of people say, "I want to take time to focus on my relationship. I want to build my relationship. I want to make that a priority. Then one day when that is taken care of, I will look at serving the world." Unfortunately, this does not work. What helps a relationship thrive, what allows two people to stay in love, to remain connected, and to sustain intimacy, is the force of love itself. Love *is* indivisible. Love is an outpouring from the divine heart into our own hearts. The more we care for humanity and for the

Earth, the more we let the river of love flow abundantly through our hearts. Love is, and must be, love for all.

The love within a relationship is the same love that we have for our partner, for our cats, for our dogs, for the animals in the world, for the poor in the world, and for those who are struggling or excluded because of race or socioeconomic conditions. It's all the same love. Love cannot be divided and cut into pieces. We cannot say we're going to just focus on our relationship. What helps a relationship survive and thrive is the amount and the intensity of love that is available. Again, we are beginning to grasp what it means that love is one and indivisible. We love our partner to the degree that we love the world. We can relate passionately to our partner to the degree that we are passionate about the pursuit of freedom, justice, peace, and solidarity in the world.

Our service to the world resources us in love. Service helps us find the ability to stay passionately in love with our partner. By serving the world, not only do we give, but we receive back at least tenfold. There is nothing that gives back more to us than service. There is nothing that has given me more in life than when I was able to reach out to someone who was struggling and offer support or solace. Those involved in humanitarian work, those who work for political and social justice, know this. It is their source of energy. So the source of energy for a couple is service as individuals and as a couple. That is what nurtures their ability to bring even greater love back to the relationship.

Love comes from the Divine. Love comes from the

divine heart. By nature, the Divine is relational. The Divine is love in relationship with itself, with the world, with the Cosmos, with this expanding Universe, with every sentient being. We are all relational beings. We cannot *not* be relational. This is who we are in our nature.

To be relational is to be engaged. For example, when our children are sick, it is a no-brainer. We relate to them in their sickness and support them because that is who we are. We are also relational with the whole planet. This is who we are. We were created as relational beings to relate in love to the entire planet. All the children on Earth are our children. We are in relationship with them. We cannot individually solve all the problems of the world but we can, individually and especially as a couple, stay in relationship with the struggle for evolution and transformation in the world. We can be cognizant and do our part. And when we stay in relationship with the world, we are in harmony with our authentic relational nature.

Also, it is the nature of love to flower into passion. Passion is not something on the side that we visit every now and then. Passion is the natural fulfillment of love. Love was created to expand into passion. Therefore, to have a loving relationship with our beloved partner means to seek and to work so that love can fully expand itself into passion.

What is fascinating is that by pursuing passion, we are confronted by all that keeps our heart locked-in and personalized. The greatest threat to a relationship is when it is personalized, when we think it is only private and just between two people.

Passion comes from a heart that is open, from a heart that wants to be as big as it can be. Passion comes from a heart that realizes it contains the whole world. Our love can only flourish if we come out of our personalized and privatized prison and open ourselves in service to the world, to the planet, and to the Divine. Our service is to divine love. We are, in essence, the great lovers of the world and the Universe. As we rediscover and claim our essence, we open the doors wide for love.

The Seven Requirements of Love
—Andrew Harvey

Chris has formulated the real principles of a new vision of evolutionary love as it now is appearing on the planet at the very moment when the planet is in extreme danger. What this vision offers humanity is a vision of coupledom, of relationship, not as a privatized escape from reality, but as the source of the fuel from which two beings united in passion can go out and become sacred activists and dedicate their inner and outer resources to helping the world. They can enjoy the fullness of divine human love in the depths of their own personal relationship, but also enjoy it in the ways that those healing depths make them powerful and strong and lucid and vibrant enough to go out into the world and pour out their gifts and resources for the transformation of the planet.

What the Divine Mother is now birthing in all those open to her is a vision of total relationship between heart, mind, body, and soul, so that through that deep sacred relationship, we can come into the unified force field of reality, become completely embodied and present, and use that inner love to express our longing to see the world transformed by justice and to protect creation. What is really at stake is this: If we continue to have a vision of relationship as purely personal, purely private, and something that we cultivate only for our own pleasure, we will keep feeding the tragic narcissism that is now ravaging the planet on every level. The real thrust and purpose and meaning and divine importance of relationship is to give us the fuel to take on the world, the passion to embrace the struggle for justice, the energy to keep on pouring ourselves out for the creation of a new world.

It is critical to remember that this crisis we are facing is a crisis in which the sacred powers of love in the human soul are being diverted by distraction, by greed, by ignorance, by the pursuit of power, so that they never irrigate the world and transform it. What is needed is a vision of evolutionary relationship as a relationship that helps us come into the real, take responsibility for it, and enact our sacred purpose with a partner, and for the world: when two lovers come together in this dynamic love consciousness, they create a transformative field of sacred energy, from which both can feed to inspire their work in reality.

There are seven requirements necessary, I believe, for this tremendously potent vision of evolutionary love to emerge in the world.

The first requirement is that both beings need to be plunged individually into a deep and passionate devotion of the Beloved, by whatever name they know the Beloved, because without both beings centering their life in God, the relationship will never be able to escape the private circle. From the very beginning it must be centered in the Divine. It must be a relationship that is undertaken in the conscious presence *of* the Divine *for* the Divine's great work in the Universe. Only a relationship that is centered in God, and that has God as the prime actor in the relationship, will be able to bear the vicissitudes of authentic love, of dealing with the challenges of life and service in the world.

The second requirement for an evolutionary love is that both beings must develop a mastery of solitude. In his *Letters to a Young Poet,* Rilke wrote: "Authentic love is where two solitudes border, protect, and salute each other." They "border" each other, they don't infiltrate each other's domain. They "protect" because they realize that the solitude that each one has is the source of inner wealth and inner revelation; they "salute" because they understand that the work of solitude, the work that goes into solitude, the heart work, the yearning, the longing, the deep contemplation of one's gifts and one's faults, is a sacred work that is the secret foundation of healthy relationship. In too many relationships in our current narcissistic model, what threatens the person most is the solitude of the other. In a true evolutionary relationship, what can exhilarate one person the most is the other's solitude, because they know that solitude has the potential to make them a billionaire of generosity, of insight, and of creativity.

The third requirement is that in a true evolutionary relationship there is an equality of power, and that equality is born out of a profound experience of the sacredness and dignity of the other person's soul. This new relationship that is trying to be given to us by the Mother is what I call the beloved-beloved relationship. One person isn't the beloved and the other only the lover. Both partners recognize in each other the unique face that God is turning to them in order to bring them the essence of divine truth, which is embodied love. From that recognition of each other as the Beloved flows a natural movement of passionate honoring and service of the other's life. This gives each person the freedom and the energy and the joy that they need to go out into the world and fulfill their destiny. This is crucial because in the past there has been a vision of inequality of power. The male has often had the power and the female hasn't. Dominant and submissive roles between two people have been seen as inevitable. Now what's emerging is the mutual recognition of holiness and sacredness expressed in tantric rapture, in an adoration and worship of the other in the core of life.

The fourth requirement follows on from the third: if you are going to have a beloved-beloved relationship, you have to center your whole being and work and evolution in God. You have to be a master of your own solitude so that you can work on what is necessary to deepen that sacred relationship of the Divine. You must also bring the sacred practice of prayer and meditation into the very core of your life, so that the whole relationship can be enfolded in a mutually shared sacred enterprise.

The fifth requirement is that both lovers completely abandon any Hollywood sentimentality about what relationships actually are. As love becomes more evolutionary and conscious, so does each lover's understanding of each other's shadow. One of the essential roles of this new love is to make each person in the relationship the safe-guarder of the other's shadow—not the judge of the other's shadow, not the denier of the other's shadow, but someone who recognizes where the other has been wounded, and safeguards and protects them with unconditional compassion without allowing themselves to be mauled or manipulated by the other. This takes an immense effort, because it takes an immense effort to understand your own shadow, and an even greater effort to face and comprehend, without illusion, denial or repulsion, the shadow of the other.

The sixth requirement is that if you are going to enter into the evolutionary process, you have to accept that it never ends, never stops unfolding. There is no end to transformation, because divine love is infinite. Evolution is fundamentally a death/rebirth cycle that repeats itself in higher and higher dimensions, and any authentic evolutionary relationship must have the courage to go through the deaths that engender the rebirths. Marion Woodman, the great Jungian analyst and pioneer of the sacred feminine, said to me, "I have had four marriages with my husband, and at the end of each marriage there was a crisis that we had to make the commitment to go through, a projection that had to die. But we stuck at it and we went through it, and the love that we know now in our eighties is the greatest and deepest love we have experienced."

The seventh principle requirement is that from the very beginning of this adventure into evolutionary love you must make the commitment for it not to be just a personal orgy, a cultivation of an oasis of private pleasure. You must engage consciously in this relationship to make you stronger, to serve the planet, to recognize that it is a relationship not only grounded in God, not only infused by sacred practice, but it is from the very beginning dedicated to making both people more powerful, more reflective, more passionately engaged with the only serious truth of our time: The world is dying, and we need a major revolution of the heart to empower everyone to step forward and start doing the work of reconstruction and re-creation that is now desperately needed.

A Socially Engaged Relationship
—Chris Saade

Let us explore what this engaged and passionate relationship looks like. First, it looks like two people coming together and attempting to develop the beloved-beloved relationship. They say to one another, "Let us develop a vision of how we can be engaged in the world, for democratic freedoms, peace, justice, and inclusion." These two people spend time, a lot of special and scheduled time, to develop a vision in which they work together for something that brings greater love and care into the world.

Second, these partners impassion their vision. They see service as a sacred prayer, not simply as an act of charity. They see their relationship as a contribution to the transformation of the world, as a sacred act of communion—the purpose of which is the flowering of humanity and the protection of the Earth. In this way, they make the choice to impassion their relationship from the fullness of their hearts, just as they would impassion their most intimate prayer to the Divine.

Third, both partners learn to embody the word *generosity*. It is such a powerful word. The ancient Romans and Greeks thought *generosity* to be the greatest ethical word. Generosity is so important because it is that which guides our bodies, minds, and hearts to flow with abundant and soulful gifts to others.

Through their engagement in the world, the couple learns to become more and more generous. By learning the essence of generosity through their service, they have so much more generosity to give to each other—because passion is fed by generosity. As human beings, we love to receive gifts—even those who protest by saying, "I don't need it" or tell the one bearing gifts: "You shouldn't have," fundamentally love gifts. It is part of our human truth. Gifts nurture our sense of being seen and loved. Look at holidays or other occasions when we receive gifts. In older traditions, any time you approached somebody who was part of royalty, you brought a gift. Coming without a gift was never considered appropriate, because a gift was a symbol of your appreciation, connection, and respect.

We learn the generosity of gifting by serving. Then we can start practicing more and more gifting in our relationship. Every day is a new day in which we can gift our partner. Sometimes the gift is material, sometimes the gift is emotional, sometimes the gift is a wonderful neck and back massage. As we give, our psyche becomes more oriented toward giving and geared away from protecting itself.

Let us talk a bit about this movement from protection to giving. A relationship has shadows. We bring to each other our great gifts but we also bring our shadows—those parts of ourselves that, because of our wounding and our genetic makeup, are not our best. This weakness or lack can sometimes be hurtful. A couple has to deal with the fact that, at some point, each will be disappointed or hurt by the other. It is normal. It is what happens in relationship. A relationship is also challenged with communication issues—a breakdown in communication, a breakdown in understanding. A relationship usually follows a cycle of breakdowns and breakthroughs. How do we deal with this cycle? How do we keep from being overwhelmed, from losing the passion and fire because of the moments of conflict and disappointment? Disappointment is a part of love that we can not get rid of. It's always going to be there. There is no way to avoid disappointment and hurt in a relationship. But there is a possibility to hold these in a way that ennobles them, and ultimately empowers the relationship.

Ralph Waldo Emerson believed that individual problems cannot be resolved by personal solutions. They need a solution that is much bigger than the personal, one that guides us beyond the realm of personalizing and isolating our lives. For a long time in the field of psychology we thought we had to find personal resolutions to our relationship problems first, and then we could become mature and face the world in a mature way. But now we know there are no ultimate personal solutions.

If the problems do not go away, the essential issue

becomes: how do we learn to relate to our problems? If we allow our personal problems in a relationship to become central, they overwhelm the relationship. They overwhelm the human psyche. We find ourselves obsessing about them day after day and our life begins to center around them. We begin to be consumed by our own personal problems, the very problems that have no ultimate solutions.

However, when we are engaged in serving the world, we come into a deeper understanding and acceptance of our personal problems, because we have a much bigger picture in which to hold them. We see our issues from an eagle's perspective. Yes, maybe you didn't get the warm hug you wanted so much this morning, but when you are engaged in the world and see the sorrow of the world and the struggle of the world, perhaps it doesn't wash away your disappointment, but it does give you a context so you can deal well with it.

Furthermore, our engagement in the world changes the focus of our psyche. We move from the focus being on our overwhelming personal issues to what we can do for the world, how we are touching other people, and how we are bringing love to the world. There's a shift in focus. We recognize that our being is rooted in solidarity. That shift in focus allows a couple to be excited, thrilled, and enriched by something they are doing together in the world, rather than obsessing about their personal disappointments. Instead of thinking that they can get rid of the disappointments and hurts, they learn how to live with them with bigger hearts, bigger psyches, and bigger minds. In doing so, they come into a fuller reflection of the Divine itself, which is love toward the whole world. When we are asked to become more like the Divine, we are asked to open up our hearts and approach our relationship problems with a huge heart. The bigger our heart, the more diversity and differences we can shelter in it. Loving and serving our Earth expands our heart. A thriving relationship needs an expanded heart.

I want to give an example of a couple I know and have worked with. They have their own regular set of disappointments. They have a beautiful connection but they also have areas where they don't connect. These two decided to get very involved in the cause of the homeless. They chose to see that cause as a sacred portal through which they could offer a wellspring of love. They trained themselves in the field and developed their passion to serve the world, devoting many weekends to their work together. Their conversations at the dinner table became more about the world, about homelessness, and about what they're able to give and what they're not able to give. Before this shared commitment, most of their discussions were about their personal disappointments with one another and what they could and could not do about them. These disappointments may still be there, but their conversations have now shifted focus toward their hopes and solutions for the world, which are larger than their individual problems. Their conversations also shifted toward the sheer enjoyment of making a difference, and doing so together, as a couple.

Out of their new conversations came more energy, more love, and more respect for one another: "This is my companion who is helping me in this meaningful project." The respect between them grew, the attraction grew, and they are now in their eighth year of relationship. Because of their shared engagement in the world they are more attracted to each other personally—emotionally, as well as sexually—than ever before. Their focus changed when their hearts became engaged and enlarged.

Illustrations of Engaged Love
—Andrew Harvey

My great friend Linda Tucker and her partner, Jason Turner, are a couple who are living this evolutionary love with passion and joy and humor through their work with the endangered white lions in South Africa. Jason understands the behavior of lions because he spent his whole life observing them. Linda is the woman whom the African shamanic tradition has selected to protect the creatures the African shamanic tradition considers the most sacred on Earth, the white lions of Timbavati.

I've been privileged to work intimately with Linda on many occasions. What I have experienced by being the close friend of both Jason and Linda is the depth of their mutual honor and mutual respect, and their celebration of the qualities that each of them bring to this enterprise. Jason brings the scientific understanding that only a long scientific training could give him. Linda brings the shamanic vision that only a profound initiation into the truth of the unified force field of nature and into the sacred identity of the white lions could have given her. The bringing together of their different gifts and their mutual celebration and mutual honor has transformed them both and given the enterprise that they're dedicated to a solidity and a groundedness which makes it extraordinarily powerful and effective in the world.

So, not only are Linda and Jason supporting each other by the immense love that they have for each other, but bringing their gifts together to serve the lions has made them a force to be reckoned with. They are a couple that stands for, in my heart, the sacred marriage, the marriage of the Divine Masculine and the Divine Feminine that is creating the Universe. Being with them and being irradiated by their love for each other and being embraced by the generosity that their love has kept alive and grown in both of them, has given me a vivid, real sense of what evolutionary love is capable of.

It's a love that is grounded in the sacred. It's a love that's grounded in the world. It's a love that's grounded in sacred purpose. It's a love that is fully embodied and sensual, and that also has profound spiritual dignity.

Linda and Jason give me visceral hope. All the more so because the more public person in their partnership is Linda, and she is a gorgeous, powerful woman. To see Jason, a gorgeous, powerful man, support and honor a gorgeous, powerful woman taking a sacred role in the world is awe-inspiring, especially because Jason doesn't lose any of his masculine dignity in doing so.

Jason is so deeply honoring of Linda's unique mission that anything that he can do to serve it is his joy. When I last saw him, just before I left Timbavati, I asked him, "Jason, How are you really?" He smiled and said, "I couldn't imagine being anywhere else, doing anything else with any other person."

I want to say here how essential it is to ground our adventure into evolutionary relationship in the Divine. The great problem with romantic love is that in our privatized, Westernized vision of romantic love, the longings that can only find satisfaction in the eternal are projected onto another fragile, difficult, complicated, wounded, and mortal human being.

This projection is initially very potent, but it is doomed to tragic disappointment. In our culture, relationships have to bear the weight of the soul's greatest longing for divine fulfillment. This means that they are threatened by all kinds of betrayal and disappointment. It's very important at the outset of this adventure into evolutionary love to realize that the true home of all of our longings, the true fulfillment of all of our desires is not in a human relationship alone.

True fulfillment streams from the relationship of the soul with the Beloved, because only the Beloved can fill the God-sized hole in our hearts. Only the Beloved can transform us completely. Once you've truly understood this and not imposed on the other a divine identity which he or she cannot sustain, then you're free to turn to the beloved and use the relationship with the Beloved to make you more compassionate, more energetic, more gentle, and more steady so that you can enjoy the timeless Beloved in the form of your human beloved, while not projecting onto your human beloved the needs and longings that only the divine Beloved can ultimately satisfy.

Without this central focus on the Beloved, you will always be in danger of compelling the person you are in love with to be God for you when he or she can only be a human divine face of God. This is important. Without understanding this subtle distinction, the new vision of evolutionary love will flounder in subtle narcissism and despair. With this knowledge, people will be given the insight, wisdom, and vision to continue working with the fragile, chaotic energies of human relationship so that more and more and more of the divine truths can permeate them, steady them, stabilize and irradiate them.

I want to really make precise to you what I believe the beloved-beloved relationship is. I will give you two grand examples and one example, from my own life. The grand examples are Shams and Rumi, and Jesus and Mary Magdalene. I have meditated on both relationships for forty years.

What I've come to understand is that Shams and Rumi, these two glorious men who fell totally, mystically in love with each other, realized a new kind of love which has influenced the entire world. The traditional version of this love has been that Shams was Rumi's master and Rumi was the disciple. Then there was another version in which they were lovers. I don't think either of these versions is true. I believe that what they really broke into was this sacred equality of mutual honoring and respect that is the key to evolutionary love. Rumi gave Shams as much as Shams gave Rumi. Rumi was the ideal receiver of Sham's shattering radiance, but there was a total gift on both sides. Rumi and Shams fulfilled each other on the highest imaginable levels of intimacy, which made each the other's beloved.

In that total equality of sharing, that total equality of self-donation, what Rumi and Shams came to experience together was the essence of embodied divine love itself. The miracle of divine love is its humility, its absolute concern for the other, it's total giving of self in honoring of the other. When two beings come into that beloved-beloved relationship, they experience that radiant humility and its ecstasy and power directly, and both are transformed together in the Divine Beloved.

The second relationship is of Jesus and Mary Magdalene. It is becoming increasingly clear, from the discovery of gnostic texts like "The Gospel of Mary" that each were the other's tantric beloved and that Jesus learned as much from Mary Magdalene as Mary Magdalene learned from Jesus. They came to each other needing each other's divine vision, divine beauty, divine strength, and divine knowledge. Without the initiation into the embodiment mysteries of the sacred feminine that only an evolved woman adept like Mary Magdalene could have given him, Jesus would never have become a fully balanced teacher incarnating the power of the sacred marriage. When this truth is recognized, a holy and wholly different and far saner vision of sacred embodied divine relationship will be at the core of Christianity. A whole horror of separation of body and soul, mind and body, sexuality and worship will be healed.

The third example is from my own life. One of my greatest friends invented a television series and then sold it and made a lot of money. She devoted herself to philanthropy and was lonely, but then met a man who was disillusioned by the business world and wanted to devote his resources and his passions to really helping. These two extraordinary people filled with passion for the world came together. I've seen them both flourish and flower on every level.

I've seen them really become a force in the philanthropic world because everybody respects them and knows that their sincerity is deep and that their energies are focused. They tune and support each other all the time. I have seen them give an inspiring example to the whole philanthropic class, which, as you know, is a very complicated, ambiguous class of people. Some are genuinely generous and some are in a big power cocktail party trying to show off.

What my two friends have done through their sacred relationship is give their world an example of what dedication really looks like. They challenge everyone in their philanthropic world to give until it hurts and to give from a place of humble, committed service. What an extraordinary legacy and how amazing the power of evolutionary love is, not only to transform us personally, but to create a powerful force for transformation in the world.

The Privatization and Evolution of Love
—A Dialogue between Chris Saade and Andrew Harvey

Chris Saade: The whole idea of evolutionary love brings us hope—hope for the building of relationships that are solid and powerful in their connection with the world, and their communion with the longing of the world. Andrew, I'd love for us to dialogue about this whole idea of the privatization/isolation of relationships.

The idea of relationship has evolved from one in which the powerful would conquer somebody else, bring them to their "cave," and imprison them within a rigid family structure. Women have suffered incredibly from this hierarchical system as did men who were not as strong physically. It was relationship as conquest.

Then it evolved into the idea of relationship as arranged. That was less destructive than conquest, but it still had its fundamental problem of inequality in decision making and high possibility of mismatches.

The third step in the evolution of relationships was when we challenged the idea of arranged marriage and defined marriage as falling in love. This was a very powerful step for humankind because love became central. It became clear to our thinking that building a family needed to be based on falling in love. Yet it was still a privatized and socially isolated idea of falling in love.

The "falling in love" step helped us evolve from the older versions, but it got stuck in a privatized, i.e. personalized idea of relationship—a relationship being an isolated island *away* from the world rather than a presence *in* the world. It is through the sacred activism of love that we are able to break out of the idea of relationship as privatization. Love-in-action reminds us that our relationships, however intimate they are, are part of the soul of the world, part of the collective struggle for peace, freedom, justice, and inclusion.

Andrew Harvey: It is clear to me that, except in some extraordinary relationships, we haven't really seen this new evolutionary love take hold yet. Conquest is clearly not the way to go because it means that there is no equality. There's no beloved-beloved relationship. Arranged marriage can work. I know this because I have lived in India and I have a great reverence for the Indian system. People who don't have exaggerated romantic expectations of one another but come to the other as a solid partner in the business of life can achieve extraordinary things together. I have seen moving and beautiful marriages over time emerge from this. But that isn't what we're talking about here, because it doesn't have this power we are celebrating of evolutionary love. This great force can only be born through being connected to God, connected to the Cosmos, and worshipping the other as the Beloved.

As you made clear, Chris, we evolved out of the traditional relationship box into trusting the heart, trusting love, and trying to build a unit around a private relationship, and, as you said, this hasn't worked either. Those who have done this have not been mature enough, have not been deeply aware enough of their own shadow, and have not been plunged deeply enough into divine worship to know what love truly is. It's not just a series of passions or a series of needs or wants. It is a primordial, sacred power. So in this privatization of relationship you have people choosing a narrow, distorted vision of what love is, then trying to live a life devoted to that vision and very often ending in disappointment, failure, or sad, bewildered compromise.

When you look at our world it's very obvious that there are dark, brilliant, coherent, and organized forces engaged in deep, destructive work endangering the planet. These powers have created in our world a perfect lethal system. They have perpetrated and concretized a societal addiction to greed; consequently, our sacred powers are wasted on an addiction to getting and spending. This addiction to greed infiltrates our private lives too. We are addicted to a privatized notion of relationship that we pursue frantically and protect anxiously. If we aren't exhausted by working for money, we're exhausted by trying to find a romantic relationship without making our relationship with the Divine the essential goal of our lives.

These constrictions mean that we don't pour our energies into social transformation, political transformation, economic transformation because we simply don't have the energy. The privatization of relationship, the capitalist enterprise, the domination of nature, and the submission of an entire world to a fundamentalism of greed all come together in an endlessly narrow divisive separatist vision that I call the "coca-coma." Which is why at this moment sacred activism is being born on the Earth. This new force of the birth, this force that brings together the passion of the mystic for God with the passion of the activist for justice; this force is the birthing force of the new humanity. To provide the fuel for this force, a new evolutionary vision of love as relationship is being graced us. Because it is the only vision that can sustain the electric and radical purpose of this emerging new humanity.

Chris Saade: Yes. It is fascinating that the electric, passionate creative force that we need and the world needs is the creative force of love—unbounded love! Passion arises from being in love with the idea of justice, in love with the idea of solidarity, and in love with the idea of peace—and also in love with the authentic truth of who we are—the freedom to be our own authenticity. To be able to keep passionate love alive, a relationship needs to be a source of energy rather than the impossible project that is handed to us: "Here you go. Go become an island. Privatize your relationship and then try to find energy in it." It is an impossible task. The couple gets more and more depressed, resulting in less and less energy for themselves and for sacred activism.

The separatist vision given to us is the perfect plan to weaken our ability to be engaged in love's sacred activism. There is also the danger that we have privatized the Divine. The idea of privatization has been taught for a long time. Now even the image of God as unbounded love has been abducted by a privatized idea of God.

Andrew Harvey: Yes.

Chris Saade: God becomes another island.

Andrew Harvey: A transcendent force, not immanent in the world and in the conditions of the world.

Chris Saade: Exactly. An island unto itself. And we become privatized islands relating to other privatized islands. Feminist thinking and feminist theology have helped us break out of this idea of privatization and realize that the Divine is inseparable from the world, the Earth and the Cosmos. The Divine is a web of relationships as we are a web of relationships. To love the Divine, to make the Divine central in our life means to make the least among us, the most deprived of their rights among us, a priority—to protect all our children, our elders, our sick, and the animals of this Earth.

God and the Divine cannot be separated from the tears of the world nor the joy of the world. Therefore, when we free ourselves from the privatized idea of the Divine and from the privatized idea of relationship, we open up to a very rich landscape. Our relationship becomes a vehicle, a sacred, wonderful, and often ecstatic vehicle through which we become intimate with the longing of life—the aspirations of the planet that we inhabit.

Andrew Harvey: It becomes a form of worship. Your relationship becomes a prayer that you offer to the Divine.

Chris Saade: Exactly.

Andrew Harvey: It goes two ways: On one hand you're saying, "I hope that the way I love you pleases the Divine who is inherent in everything," on the other hand, you're praying that the relationship will give you such vigor, such strength, such joy that all your dreams of serving the world will be fulfilled. You have the backing. You have the support—from the Divine and from your partner.

Wherever I travel in the world, I meet brilliant and brave people doing extraordinary work, but most of them are alone. And they are alone because they can't find the people who want them to do the work that they long to do in the world, the people who know how to support them. The choice for so many sacred activists at the moment is doing the work for which they feel destined and which will contribute to the transformation of the planet, or looking for a relationship. Not, however, the hurtful, exhausting, debilitating relationships of their past. What is the solution? There's only one solution: Everybody moves to a new level of love. Stop privatizing God. Stop separating yourself from the world. Realize that love is joining with this primordial passion force and is here, with you and for you, to transform the world.

Chris Saade: Exactly. It is so, so important to understand what is the source of love. People think that the person they found is the source of love. We discover a new person and for the first three months we find so much loving within us. The "wanting" of them is so strong that we think, "Hey, I have it. I can maintain this." But six months or nine months later, after the romantic phase of the relationship, people lose that power. They say, "What's wrong with my partner? What's wrong with me? What's wrong with us?" But it's neither your partner nor you. It is that you haven't gone to the source of love, to the Divine who is love unbounded, love for the journey of the world. It is the Divine who is standing with the poor. It is the Divine who is grieving for the oppressed children. It is the Divine who works for justice, and consistently calls us to love.

In my thirteen years of humanitarian work in Lebanon I experienced this. The love that we desire from our partner—yes, they can give us some of that. But, at least for a lot of us, the powerful flow of love's river comes from the Divine through the world, through the people we are helping. It is amazing how much love there is. These children, for example, who are abandoned, when you go to them and you hold them and you give them a moment of solace. Maybe you can't change their life, but you can hold that child next to your heart, and you give them food and love for one evening. The love they give back to you is amazing. It's a love that can last a lifetime. I still remember eyes that looked at me in war-torn situations. They looked at me with gratitude or kindness or saying thank-you and I still remember it as if it were happening right now. So we have to remember the real source of love. Service is not something we do when we have time to do it, it is the wellspring of our being. Out of that primordial source of love, we fill our hearts and then can give and maintain passion for the beloved with whom we chose to bond.

Andrew Harvey: Yes, this is so important. Service is what actually keeps the springs of love bubbling with fire. Linda and Jason would never have the love they have if they were not in love with the lions and what they symbolize. They have something so much larger than their personal relationship at the core of their relationship. That is what keeps it fresh and vibrant and exciting to them and to others who participate in what they are creating. This is what they are bringing in and what they are making available to the world.

Chris Saade: Exactly. Through the evolutionary vision of relationship, we experience a breakthrough in our consciousness. The evolutionary vision of relationship also provides us with many very practical tools. And I mean very practical. In some of my counseling and coaching, when people are in a very difficult, stuck place, I will say to them, "Okay, just freeze the problem for a bit." They might be thinking they need to separate but I tell them to go and spend a day or a week of service and then come back and we'll talk. When they do come back it's a different level of dialogue. They come back energized. They come back feeling that love has touched them through those they have helped. They come back with a sense of perspective about who they are in relationship and about the problem with their relationship. Of course that is not a quick fix but it does help the couple approach their issues from an expanded mind and enlarged heart.

Andrew Harvey: They probably come back with a deep sense of respect for each other, because the tragedy of the privatized version of relationship is that we get mired in each other's shadows and each other's difficulties and disappointments. We forget that the person we love is also capable of doing wonderful, glowing, passionate things in the world. When you see them, you realize, "Oh my God, how amazing he or she is."

Chris Saade: There's nothing sexier than seeing our beloved doing an act of service in the world. Because what we see is the splendor of the Divine in him or her.

Andrew Harvey: We see the true beauty. We see why we fell in love with them in the first place.

Chris Saade: We see the Mary in them, we see the Christ in them. We see the Krishna in them. We are turned on by that. I say to couples, "Whatever issue you have, you are going to have it all your life." Then I say, "This is the moment to fire me as your therapist or as your coach, because I'm not going to tell you that you will be rid of your problem. What I can tell you is that there is a way you can put it in perspective—have the issue become a respected authentic difference rather than an ongoing hurt."

Respect, admiration, desire, and love of the other can grow much more intense and much larger than the disappointment and the problems. How? By each person claiming their authenticity as well as their humanity, as it was designed to be from the very beginning, i.e. a mirroring of the loving, giving, generous image of the Divine—unbounded freedom and unbounded sense of solidarity!

Andrew Harvey: People have tried to do this within a narrow family context and often achieve amazing things. You see them being able to get over their personal difficulties by really loving their family. But what we're all being asked by this great crisis to consider goes far beyond the family context. It isn't enough just to love your partner, or your children, or your grandchildren, or your family structure because that can become an obsessive hiding from the pain of the world.

What's essential to understand is that we're in a world which is falling totally apart, in which the whole future of humanity and a great deal of nature is at stake. We can no longer afford any kind of purely private love because that purely private love will keep us from facing the full implications and rising to the challenge of where we are in history.

Three things are required of the evolutionary lover in this crisis. First, that that lover faces the world crisis head-on and feels it. Secondly, that in feeling it, they allow their intense heartbreak to come out and not hide from it. Then they realize that the true meaning of their life is in following that heartbreak to find a mission to do something about this terrifying crisis. The third requirement is that their trust is not in a personal relationship alone, but much more importantly it is grounded in the transcendent immanent Godhead in the Father/Mother so that their whole being is receptive to the energies of divine joy and divine love. When those three things come together they have the power to propel the greatest leap in human relationship deep into evolutionary love.

There is a line by Rumi which goes to the core of everything: "Let divine passion triumph and rebirth you in yourself." Allow yourself to experience the core of God that is this infinite power, divine passionate love that is creating the entire Cosmos, the love of the Beloved exploding as the Big Bang in the whole Cosmos. Experience that and let it triumph. Let it take you over. Let it burn in every cell of your being and rebirth you in your true self, which is not the privatized, neurotic self, but the divine human self that is at home in the whole Universe and in love with the whole Universe. Then from that place, love another human being on the same radical journey, and see what happens. Why shouldn't you live with your sacred partner what Shams and Rumi lived together, or Jesus and Mary Magdalene—an embodied human divine love that is at once a personal revelation and the source of a new vision of action in the world. As Marcus Aurelius said, "Don't just honor great beings. Become one yourself."

Chapter 2
Passion

Spiritual Passion
—Andrew Harvey

You cannot have an evolutionary vision of love without an authentic, powerful, inspiring vision of God as evolutionary. The two go together. One of the greatest tragedies of our long religious exploration is how we have abandoned the passionate, ever-becoming, creative side of the Divine—the relational side, the experimental side, the side that is inventing new possibilities at every moment—in favor of a static, ethereal and privatized vision of God and of enlightenment. This old vision of the Divine as separate, as peaceful, as purely transcendent, as outside the world, to be connected with through the loneliness of the achieved solitude of the seeker, is now being detonated by the single greatest force in the Universe, which is the Divine Feminine. The Mother has seen that unless she returns to us in full embodied majesty, outrage, passion, and beauty, we will not be able to evolve into the next stage of our evolution, because our evolution depends on being united with the passionate force of creative love that is the Mother's supreme nature and the gift of the Mother to us.

What we now need is an evolutionary vision of God as the sacred marriage between opposites, the dance of opposites in the One. Unless the full majesty of the transcendent Father and the full majesty of the embodied Mother are brought together and felt and experienced together, we will never be completely human and never be completely divine. We will never know love as the primordial, evolutionary force of the Universe, grounded in, and emanated from, the eternal light. This is the force that we must align with in our love relationships to help us evolve the Divine in us and the Divine in the world.

Four lines by the great Hindu mystic, Kabir, who lived in Benares, India, in the fifteenth century, express this dynamic, evolutionary relationship with the evolutionary force of God. Kabir had a complete realization of the Father/Mother beyond religion and knew himself born into embodied, divine humanity in the center of life. He wrote these four lines, which, for me, are the ultimate celebration of the evolutionary love force. He says,

> *My Father is the Transcendent Absolute,*
> *and my Mother is the Embodied Godhead,*
> *and I am their Divine Child,*
> *dancing for them both on their burning dance floor.*

When you really unpack those lines, you see and feel what a complete human divine life is. First Kabir says, "My father is the Transcendent Absolute"—the infinite light, the unborn and undying light that is the source of all things, while always transcending them. Knowing this "Father" side of the Divine is to know that in your depth you are one with its deathless, serene and blissful consciousness. Knowing this only, however, is not enough. It is one side of the relationship to God, and it is foundational and essential; it's the side, as I've said, that brings you great peace. But without great passion, peace will make you passive, just as without great peace, great passion will make you hysterical and deranged.

Kabir goes on to say, "My Mother is the Embodied Godhead." The Mother is the force of radiant love passion that arises from the heart of the Godhead and creates the Universe and lives in the Universe in all of its particulars. When you acknowledge the Father, the origin, as the eternal, spacious, peaceful light, but also know that's not enough to enter into your full human divinity, what's required then is to plunge into the molten, fiery, creative passion of the Mother to unite that passion with the great peace. Then you become what Kabir says he is in the third line: "I am their Divine Child. Dancing for them both on their burning dance floor."

Evolutionary love is a dancing with the essential nature of this evolutionary God. It is at once profoundly peaceful and profoundly passionate, deeply solitary, and absolutely engaged with relationship on every level. These paradoxes come together in the nature of The One.

When Kabir says, he is dancing on the Mother/Father's burning dance floor, you get the edge, the excitement, the adventure, the madness, and the urgency of the authentic evolutionary adventure, because as Kabir makes clear, this dimension we must live it out in is burning. It's burning in time, it's burning in suffering, it's burning in endless change. And it's continually vanishing, so unless we commit ourselves urgently to embody these paradoxes, these opposites, the dance floor will burn away before we can claim and enact our truest, most liberated life.

What Kabir is giving us in these four lines is the image of where sacred relationship is truly born, through unity of peace and passion. As I've said, and I cannot say it often or richly enough, we will not be able to get to the authentic, empowering, passion-inducing, passion-inspiring vision of an evolutionary God unless we embrace the full Sacred Feminine as well as the true Sacred Masculine. There cannot be a marriage that builds the sacred power of the Universe in our life without a full return of the power, beauty, ecstasy, and intensity, of the love of the Mother for everything that she has created out of herself, because she lives within everything that she has created.

The great gift of this return of the Mother is passion, and it is the crucial need of our time. The patriarchal traditions have demonized passion as part of their extinction of the Divine Feminine. This degradation of the Divine Feminine has made those who experience passion, and who want to express passion, feel as if they are not holy. They are called "crazy," "hysterical," because what the patriarchy wants is a privatized god, an off-planet god to whom you can attune your whole being peacefully while serving the death machine that the patriarchy has created all over the world.

The return of the passion of the Mother, that is at once a passion for life and a passion for the service and work of healing compassion and justice that protect life, makes available to the human race both a revolutionary energy of empowered protest, an energy of "No!" to all the forces that are killing life, and a vast, creative "Yes!" to all the forces of divine tenderness and passion that are now trying to flood us, to help us wake up out of our coca-coma and galvanize our inner lives, galvanize our relationships, so that we can step up to the great task of saving the human race from extinction and enabling the great plan of God to go forward.

When divine passion is released and experienced at the heart of authentic evolutionary relationship and married to the passion burning at the heart of sacred activism—the passion for justice, for the preservation of the creation, for the birth of a humanity united by respect and compassion and embrace of diversity—all the now scattered and divided powers of love will come into unity and birth in all those initiated by grace into the power of this marriage an unstoppable, revolutionary, all-transforming force that, even at this late, tragic moment, can transform apocalypse into the birthing-ground of a new world.

Transcendent and Immanent Passion
—Chris Saade

Passion is the fulfillment of love. Passion is the celebration of life and the divine source of life, transcendent and immanent. Passion is unborn and undying. It is the spirit in us that nothing can destroy, the part of us that is fully connected and one with that core of us—the core that is our unique individual authenticity and the core that burns and struggles for democratic freedom and justice, for ecological sanity, for solidarity, and for inclusion.

Passion is also the great promise of this evolutionary relationship. The idea of two people coming together consciously wanting to create a beloved-beloved relationship, and wanting their relationship be a dance with the world and its struggles, so it can give love to the world, receive love from the world, and thrive through that fulfilling cycle of giving and receiving. That is the promise. Of course, there will be shadows, disappointment, and losses, but the promise is that it is possible to dance love, to enjoy love, to feel the ecstasy of love. It is possible to know and support our partner in her or his authenticity, to believe that our partner in their unique authenticity deserves our love and passion, and to know that we deserve to be loved with passion. That is the essence of an empowered relationship that can withstand the oppressive structures and institutions in the world and be a voice for love.

Passion, in that sense, is sacred. It is born from a calling to serve the world from the Divine, from an indivisible love. We cannot love the Divine without loving what the Divine loves. The Divine loves the grass, the water, the planet Earth, and all of us. But we have been contaminated (and unfortunately this includes any psychotherapy that denies or overlooks the crucial importance of authenticity and the relationship between the flowering of authenticity and the pursuit of love's social activism) with this idea of gradualism—I take care of myself first, then I take care of my family, then my finances, and then one day, I'll do something useful. Authenticity, love, passion, and global solidarity are states of being that are interdependent, consistently interacting, and interpenetrating.

Now I want to bring in Abraham Maslow. I have tremendous respect for Maslow. I have studied his work and I think he's one of the geniuses of our psychological field. But he presented a triangle—the triangle of self-fulfillment, of self-realization—that has, unfortunately, been perceived in ways that damaged our psychological thinking. In his model, the self-fulfillment triangle begins with survival and safety as the first layer, then evolves into physical and relationship needs. Finally, on the top of the triangle, if you are lucky enough to reach there, is the need to be philanthropic, to help others and serve the world. This triangle has been interpreted quite rigidly by some and has negatively permeated both psychological thinking and spiritual thinking.

This must be challenged because it has led to the privatized idea of relationship: "Let me take care of my private needs first, and then hopefully after I can do something for the world." A more authentic and inspiring model, I believe, should start with passion for the world. Once there is passion for the world, we are in companionship with the divine energy and we can then attend to our physical needs, relational needs, and everything else. The passion for others, the passion for the world, and the passion for each other is the starting point, not the end point. Most of those who have survived horrendous circumstances know that what helped them rebuild their lives was a vision or a sense of life that went much further than attending to their physical needs. That greater perception of what life was about involved taking care of physical and emotional needs, for sure, but it galvanized them and awakened their dormant and undefeated strength in ways that irradiated their souls and hearts.

A passionate love for the world helps us break away from the idea of the privatized personal self. It's that force that opens us up to a vision of a global self, i.e. who we really are: global beings. I love how in the Christian tradition, Jesus is perceived as the lover of the world—the one who holds the world in his heart.

The gospel narrative calls on us to all grow into the image of a defiant and most loving Christ—to become like Christ, Christ who is a global self. There is no Jesus as an individualized, personal, static self. Jesus was exuding love for the world. In that tradition, we are asked to become like Christ, to break out of the personalized self that suffocates us and become a global self in one body, in one reality. Passion is the love-energy that allows the shell of the personalized self to break open. In that sense, passion frees our spirit to become itself and to fulfill its destiny. What we are growing toward is a strong individual sense of authenticity, one that is free, staunch, straightforward, yet at the same time, aware of its roots in the soul of the world—thus abundantly generous in its solidarity of heart and mind.

It is essential to remember that we are people of free will. We can choose to reject passion or we can choose to accept passion. Passion is nothing less than the fruition of love, love deepening in us, love going into our roots, love emerging from our heart. Passion is seeing the world through the eyes of love, and thus in our relationship seeing our partner through the eyes of that burning love. There is a choice here. We have to choose—choose to make love primordial in our life, choose to allow love to flourish into passion, and choose to offer that passion to the world and to our partner. Our partner needs our passion, like the world needs our passion, like we need the passion of our partner. We are beings who are made to hold the great fire of love. We were created that way. We were created to be mirrors of the love of the Divine. We were created to thrive in the fire of love. We were created to know love as a burning fire of adoration, to adore our partner, to adore our children, and to adore the world we live in. We are beings of adoration and anything less than that creates an endemic depression in us because we are not living the life that we were created to live. We were not created to languish in lukewarm emotions. We were not made to be tepid. Passionate love is how our hearts grow and our health becomes the best it can be. We were created to love animals with the fullness of our heart. We were created to love the children of the world. That's who we are. We are unbelievably loving individuals but we have to allow that love to come out, to choose it.

A very important aspect of passion is tenderness. Passion is fire, but it is also the deep water of tenderness. Passion allows the flowering of a daring intimacy. Through the communion of intimacy, passion initiates the sparks of fire as well as the ripening of soothing words, tears, and smiles of tenderness. Fire and tenderness are both absolutely necessary for love. Through the temerity of our hearts, because love is always a temerity, passion mediates both.

If I choose passion, I have to realize that passion is going to redraw my life. The passion within me is inviting this river coming from the heart of the Godhead. My life is going to be transformed. There is a great sense of surrender that must happen—it is a surrender to the truth of my humanity.

I must let the passionate love of my heart write my life rather than letting it be written as a banal script in a small book. And when I let the great love write my life, I have to surrender to the truth of who I am. I have to give up control. This surrender progressively liberates me from victimization, the dark sense that I have of myself, that I am victimized by the world or victimized by circumstances. Through my authentic passion I can realize power and peace. There is a great deal of peace in true passion. (Later, I will discuss psychological differences, which are many, between passion and compulsion.) In passion, there is the great peace and great power that help me realize I don't have to control my own authentic nature; I don't need to control the authenticity of my beloved; I don't have to control the world. I don't even have to control my story. And I don't have to be victimized. I can free myself from the idea of being victimized, of believing that I am a person devoid of the ability to impact the world.

Passion tells us that every one of us is a co-creator of the beauty of love—in our immediate lives, where we live, where we work, in our town, or in our village. Right where we are, passion reminds us that we are co-creators of miracles. And the greatest miracle of all is our ability to communicate love and receive love in ways that are rich, full, and free of the limits that we put on ourselves.

The Transformative Power of Passion
—Andrew Harvey

Passion is like the force that splits the atom. It splits the atom of the privatized self to release the nuclear energy of dynamic love in action.

Anyone who's been through an experience of either divine or human passion, or both, knows that passion annihilates the small self and births you into the fire energies, the universal cosmic fire energies of a much vaster self. It is peaceful, but it is also wild, wildly loving, and wildly hungry to see justice done. You cannot awaken to the Mother's love for everything that she has created without also awakening to the Mother's heartbreak at the agony and injustice and cruelty and madness of what we are doing to everything She's created. You cannot awaken to the Mother's truth without waking up to the Mother's urgency to see love, justice, compassion, and harmony put into action so that the fullness of her gifts to us can be known and so that the fullness of our potential to evolve into divine human beings can be realized.

It is essential that we truly understand the nature of this Father/Mother passion. What characterizes the divine passion is that the fiery energy of divine passion arises out of profound peace and surrender. One of the ways in which our passion is policed by the patriarchy is that it's demonized as irrational, hysterical, and as a sure-fire road to burnout. But this is not the divine passion we're talking about. The Hindu mystics give us a beautiful image: The Father, they say, is the Transcendent Absolute, a diamond. The Mother is the shining of the diamond, the brilliant force that radiates from the great peace of the Father.

One of the things you discover as you cultivate divine passion in yourself is that if it isn't embedded at its core in a great spacious peace and silence, it will burn out. If it is embedded in this spaciousness, it will never burn out because it flowers effortlessly from it. Just as the Mother's great creative energy flowers effortlessly from the great transcendent peace of the Father.

An image for this kind of divine passion could be something like this: Imagine a big candle with a wonderful blazing wick. The wick will only continue to burn if there's a steady supply of calm, golden wax. Anyone who wants to cultivate divine passion will also need to cultivate the divine spaciousness and the divine peace so their passion can be as purified of neurosis and rage and anger and trauma and wounded-ness as possible. Only then can it spring straight from the heart of God in the most potent way.

This passion, as I keep emphasizing, is the supreme gift of the Divine Feminine. Emanating from the great peace, it creates the whole Universe, propels, guides, lives in and as the whole process of evolution, and continually destroys and recreates everything. This infinite passion-force is known by many names in the traditions. It's called *shakti* in Hinduism, the Holy Spirit in Christianity. My favorite name for it comes from the Persian, *ishq*.

When I say the word *ishq, ishq, ishq*, I feel the force of this vast cosmic energy rising up through my whole being. Uniting my heart, my mind, my body, the ground, the sky. I feel a great golden column of fire that rushes up and down my whole being, electrifying together and in dynamic harmony all my spiritual centers, and connecting me directly both to the transcendent light and the tiniest quarks and nutrinos in the core of matter.

In one of his gretest poems, Rumi describes the effects and power of this force with matchless intensity and precision:

> *Passion burns down every branch of exhaustion:*
> *Passion is the supreme elixir that renews all life.*
> *So don't sigh heavily, your brow bleak with boredom,*
> *Dare to look for passion, passion, passion, passion.*
> *Futile solutions deceive the force of passion*
> *They're bandits who extort money through lies,*
> *So run, my friends, from all false solutions*
> *Let divine passion triumph and rebirth you in yourself.*

Look at Rumi's first line, "Passion burns down every

branch of exhaustion." Once you connect with this endless flow of fierce, love energy coming from the God that creates everything, it is always available to you to renew and exhilarate you. It's like discovering the source of electricity in the house; you take the plug of your life and you're able to connect it into the socket that can provide the infinite electricity of *ishq*, the Holy Spirit.

In his second line, Rumi gets to the core of truth: "Passion is the supreme elixir and renews all things." In the Christian tradition this passion is known as the Holy Spirit, the ecstatic love force that connects the Creator and the creation. That fire, that *ishq*, that Holy Spirit, is the fire of divine passion that is birthing the Universe afresh at every second. This fire that is blazing in the rose. This fire is the green shimmer of the grass. This fire dances in the eyes of two friends connecting passionately about something they care deeply about. This fire, the Holy Spirit, is the supreme alchemical force of the Universe. Everything is created from it, everything is evolved from it, everything is sustained by it, and everything is endlessly renewed by it.

When I was a little boy, I read a book *She*, by Rider Haggard, which I loved. It is a story about an explorer who finds this electrifyingly beautiful African Queen in the middle of nowhere. He discovers that she is immortal and that she stays immortal by going to a cave in the mountains where she bathes in a cataract of fire. She goes into the core of the fire and comes out with her eternal youth and beauty blazing. It's a crazy story, but what the author is talking about is what Rumi knows and what His Holiness the Dalai Lama exemplifies. He's eighty years old and yet he's the most energetic, sweet, playful, childlike person in any room, because he has renewed himself incessantly in the supreme elixir of his compassion for humanity, and his endless desire to serve all beings.

In his third line, Rumi says, "So don't sigh heavily, your brow bleak with boredom." Don't side with boredom and cynicism. Don't go there because if you choose the ironic stance, or the victim stance, or the helpless stance, or the paralyzed stance, not only are you locking yourself away in your own self-created prison, but you are missing the supreme gift of life, which is to be grounded in the transcendent knowledge of your unborn, deathless origin that enables you to live out the great passion of the Mother for all things in the terms of your own personality, relationships, and life.

We have been invited onto the burning dance floor of life to partake of something of the full nature of God, to know that we are eternal, and to know too that we are evolving in time and through time with the glory and the passion of the Mother. To bring these two forms of divine knowledge together and experience them together is to enter into the great evolutionary transformation of the Universe.

That's our task now. To do this with absolute concentration on every level. As Rumi's fourth line says, "Dare to look for passion, passion, passion." Our task as evolutionary lovers is to dare to look for passion and continue through sacred practice and surrender to deepen that holy passion, so in the end it can triumph and rebirth us in our true self—the true self we discover not only in the divine peace of being, but also in the divine passion of service that is born from the fire of the Mother, the force of endless evolution.

The next stage of evolution will be born, I am convincd, from the marriage of the deepest personal authenticity—the authenticity we uncover, sustain and encourage in evolutionary relationship—with the outpouring of our unique gifts and resources in sacred activism. In those in whom this marriage takes place, serving the world becomes not an expression of duty—let alone of shame or guilt—but the continual overflowing of an inner lavishness of soul, a lavishness that grows ever more abundant as the love and ecstasy that fuel it become ever more completely suffused by the force of *ishq,* "that divine fire fountain" as Rumi writes, "that is always leaping from the core of your heart, and that is secretly fed from the One's infinite blazing light ocean."

The Energy of Passion
—Chris Saade

It is that passionate giving of ourselves, while being grounded in the peace of our connection with the unborn and the undying—i.e. the eternal in us, the infinite in us, the power in us—that existed at the time of the Big Bang and that will exist into the future. Within us we have the power to fuel our journey to the dream of love, a consciousness of peace, justice, and solidarity.

It is in passion and passionate service where our energy is regenerated. Passion is the source of energy. And, it's the same thing for a relationship. A relationship regenerates its energy of love, its romantic energy, sexual energy, and spiritual energy through offering its authentic passion to the world.

By inviting the passionate love of the Divine to abide in the center of our relationship as a passion for service to the world, the energy of love is regenerated. This is what we have come to understand on an evolutionary level. Without it, we cannot overcome the tremendous difficulty of relationship building. That is a crucial point. Unfortunately, this is not taught in psychological training.

It is extremely important to make the distinction between passion and compulsion or obsession. A lot of people speak about times in their life when they were obsessed with something, or they had a compulsion towards something and how it ended badly. A compulsion is a pull toward a rigid goal and we are laser focused on a specific result—unyielding and unbending on its form. In other words we refuse to be flexible and open to multiform results. This rigidity becomes an obsession. Compulsion does not necessarily include love. In compulsion there is also a sense of being right: "I'm correct and this is how it needs to be." When we act out of compulsion, we do not act out of the desire of our heart (an intentional, authentic choice), but rather from an unconscious dictate pulling us toward a rigid goal. In contrast, a genuine passion is authentic to us. Our true passions affirm the authenticity of our personality. They do not negate our authenticity. A compulsion easily violates the truth of our personality and heart desires. A passion is an expression of love and the result of an intentional heart choice. We have no choice in a compulsion. In passion we choose to surrender to our authentic creative power. Although, we have to acknowledge that if we dig deep into our compulsions, we can find the seed of a genuine passion that has been corrupted by toxic thinking and thus has gone awry.

The passion of the Divine, the passion of the heart, is very different than compulsion in its manifestation.

Passion follows a certain vision, but its goal is not the ultimate aim. Its aim is the outpouring of love, while pursuing that goal.

Nietzsche spoke beautifully about passion. He invited us to be passionate without the need to be right and knowing that we do not have the ultimate truth. Passion is an outflowing of love with the realization that none of us has the full truth. I don't have the full truth, but I still want to open wide this river of love to come through me without a sense of being right or being correct. I want to offer, knowing that in my offering there'll be mistakes that I will make. I'm okay with that, because I don't have to hold myself to the unhealthy standard of perfection of the ultimate truth. This distinction between compulsion and the passion of love is critically important.

Another essential distinction between compulsivity and passion is that passion is not based on self-violation. There is a refrain I often hear, "Well, you know I've spent a lot of my life giving, giving, giving, and I'm just burned out. Now I just need to stop and take care of myself." I hear a lot of that in my coaching work, and it comes from a mistaken understanding of passion. In passion, we give from what is authentic in us to give. If we give only out of a sense of duty, a sense of, "If I don't do it, who else will?" we violate our spirit and our authenticity. Obligation is not passion. It's a sense of self-sacrifice and will burn us out and send us to the opposite extreme: "I just want to take care of myself."

If you give out of what you authentically love (meaning not giving what is not authentic to you), this regenerates your energy. You don't have to burn out. To the contrary, you will build up more and more stamina. This is very important, and we will discuss it more fully later—our spirit has a particular authenticity. I have to know my spirit intimately and then only give out from my authenticity. We need to respect the outline of our being, honor its inner wealth as well as its necessary limitations, for it is our limitations and our lacks that forge our gushing sources of generosity. One does not exist without the other.

This means I have to come and say to you, my very good friend, Andrew Harvey, "There are seven or eight things I cannot give you, but there are one or two things that I can give you and I want to give them to you fully and generously. I want to flood you with what I can give you." So passion involves the ability to say, "No, that's not what my authenticity is about. My spirit doesn't do this, and it doesn't do that." But when it comes to what it does do, it does it fully. It is the great no that allows the great yes. The path of negation is sacred and essential for the outpouring of authentic love.

Passion has to be based on the authentic and not on a sense of self-sacrifice and self-violation. This is tremendously important within relationships. Relationships can easily lose their fire—romantic and sexual—if partners lose touch with their authenticity. The authentic is the ground of their generosity. There is a love that is pouring through our millions of years of evolution. The Divine is flooding us with its love so we can continue that evolution and build the consciousness of freedom, justice, solidarity, and peace. We have to bring the flame of Divine love into our relationships. Out of that flame grows emotional, romantic, and sexual love. Also, this is a love that regenerates and renews itself with the passing of years. There is more passion and more desire available in the heart even as people grow older and bodies start to transform. The couple practicing passionate love will find more and more energy available to them. We are part of a circle that flows from the Divine to the world and from the world to the relationship. Then the relationship flows back to the Divine, which takes us back to the world and the world fires us up again.

The image I have when I come to pray, is one of surrendering to what the Divine created me to be: an agent of love on all levels. In praying, I am saying, "Yes, Thy will be done. I will be what I was made to be. I will be the truth of my authenticity offered to the world in great solidarity."

Ask yourself, before going to sleep, "Was I, today, a voice for those who are not being heard? Did I stand for justice today? Was I passionate for a world of peace and democratic freedoms? Even in a small way?" That is very, very big. Because that small way has a powerful energy in it; it has the presence of divine love.

The Ultimate Aim of Passion
—A Dialogue between Andrew Harvey and Chris Saade

Andrew Harvey: Chris, I love your distinction between passion and compulsion, and I love your warning about confusing passion with blame or duty or self-sacrifice, because it cannot be divine passion if it isn't free, if it isn't freely and lavishly given out of a generosity that sacred practice and the experience of evolutionary love incessantly expands.

I want to make two other observations. Many people confuse passion with an overt emotionalism. This is neurotic human passion and it can be darkly exciting, but it doesn't have anything to do with the noble grounded passion that you hear, for example, in the music of Beethoven, or you read in the great poetry of Rumi, or you experience when you're being flooded by the majesty of what Shakespeare reveals in the great tragedies. This isn't extreme emotionalism, it is direct, blazing initiatory contact with a primordial force.

It is very important that people realize that each of us expresses this direct contact in different ways. Chris, you and I are expressive people, dramatic people. You and I enjoy the exuberance of the theater of divine love and the dance.

But there are people who are just as passionate as we are, but who express that passion in a calmer, quieter, and more down-home way. A lot of animal rights people that I know, for example, are extremely shy people. In their introversion, they've connected with the silent agony of the animals, and in their service, they bring the sweetness and tenderness of that shyness into how they interact with the animals, and also into how they present the pain of the animals to the world.

It's important to realize that everyone's passion is different. We can learn how to be passionate from Rumi and Shakespeare and Beethoven, and of course from the Source of passion, the Beloved, but we still have to be passionate in our own unique way, from our own unique self.

Chris Saade: The expression of passion will be different according to the authenticity of each person. It might be dramatic or theatrical or contained, but there is an inner knowing about it. The person will know that they are standing in the space of passion, one that that is surging through their heart and authenticity.

Andrew Harvey: They'll be in joy and know what Blake meant when he wrote, "Energy is eternal to light."

Chris Saade: They will know their great joy and they will know grief—for life is always paradoxical. But they will know they are in life abundant, and they will be propelled to give because passion is something so big it cannot be contained. It cannot be privatized.

Andrew Harvey: I want to explore here a remark made by the extraordinary French clown, Marcel Marceau. He said, "Passion is a long patience." When I first read that, I think I was in my twenties, I thought, "What on Earth does he mean?" But as I've grown, I've understood just how profound his statement is.

If you are in a relationship and you are not serving your own deep divine evolution, and the divine evolution of the person that you love, you will never know divine passion. Divine passion isn't simply the outpouring of one's self towards another, and the receiving of the outpouring of the other. Divine passion is also a commitment to the evolution of the other. It is a passionate commitment of the soul to the flowering of the unique self of the being you are privileged to be in relationship with—whatever that entails for you.

Two people who are deeply committed to the passion of the Divine must be deeply committed to serving each other's divine evolution with total concentrated passion, which entails deep patience, because without that commitment to patience, the fire of the passion will run out.

When I interviewed Maria Callas at the end of her life, she said something about passion, which I've never forgotten. "When I sing, one-half of my mind is utterly focused, and the other half of my mind is utterly gone." These two things that Marcel Marceau and Maria Callas said have really haunted me, and I think that they are the core of relationship. What Callas is talking about is what people need in their deep emotional, spiritual, and sexual relationship with each other.

First, they need to be completely present at this moment, in this moment, with the fullness of the other person. Totally focused on their own depths and on the depths of the other. This requires an immense effort of conscious presence, conscious alignment, conscious outpouring, and conscious deep contemplative, compassionate understanding. Alongside that, they also need to know how to enter the completely fresh lunacy of the moment, to be abandoned to the moment, to be surrendered to the moment, because something new is born every moment, which will be missed if they're not totally open to it. You will not be able to give birth to what's trying to be born if you don't have these faculties of precision and clarity and presence.

What passion is inviting us to, is a marriage at the deepest level, of the highest clarities of the masculine with the wildest and profoundest compassion passion energies of the feminine. They need to come together so that we can live our truth.

Chris Saade: That is so true. Passion is paradoxical in nature. It lives in paradox. It's the understanding and acceptance of paradox that allows passion to be generated and sustained—to be receptive, and totally open to the wildness.

Andrew Harvey: You can only surrender to the wildness if you are calm and clear. Otherwise, the wildness intimidates you. Callas can only sing the way she does because she's done a hell of a lot of work to train her voice. She worked sixteen hours a day for twenty years to get her voice to a place where she can abandon herself to the music and know that her voice will carry it. That's what we have to do in our personal relationships. The instruments of ourselves that we're abandoning to passion can be trusted because they have been clarified, they've been purified.

Chris Saade: I fully agree. Passion demands a commitment to a life of growth, a life of tuning and honing our authenticity and its force within us. Passion is always supportive of the evolution of the other. In my experience leading workshops for several decades, when people are asked to look at their passion, they struggle with the privatization trap. They start thinking about their passion, but their passion shrinks as it is privatized.

Let's say some have a passion to paint, or for music, or a passion for the mountains. To be developed and sustained, the passion of the heart must ultimately express itself as a passion to serve. An authentic passion will gift us with strength, pleasure, and meaning. A mature and developed passion will give us pleasure— for pleasure is very important and is holy—but at some point that passion needs to express itself as solidarity.

What is your passion to serve? If it is through painting, how does your work in some way and at some time speak to justice, to solidarity, to preservation of the natural world? If you write songs, are there some that speak out against homophobia, the abuse of animals, or the degradation of the environment? If your creative passion is from the heart, it will serve your partner and it will serve the world. If your passion is the mountains, how can your communion with the mountains at some time become a powerful inspiration for others.

There is an evolutionary lift when we ask the question, "What cause will the passion in me serve?" It will still be painting, or singing, or bicycling, or whatever it is, but it will ultimately go toward impacting others, toward supporting. Authenticity, pleasure, all merging with service.

Andrew Harvey: I love what you're saying, Chris. Passion is a long work as well as a long patience. Let's take gardening. If all you do when you're gardening is simply enjoy gardening, that's already something. But if you realize that you're entering into a relationship with the tragically endangered Earth, then your gardening, if you really love it, will take you into a radical concern for the health of the environment that can lead you, if you're brave and honest enough, to environmental activism.

What we're really inviting people to do is to identify their passion, to work with it so as to embody it at the deepest levels, and to work at expanding it, so that its true, all-embracing nature can be experienced, so that you can come to the hidden mission in the core of that passion and dedicate it to the transformation of the world. Divine passion, the passion at the core of your most authentic self, the passion to fulfill the task your authentic self reveals to you, and the passion to serve the world, not from guilt or duty, but from sacred lavishness of being, sacred exhuberance—these all interpenetrate and birth in you through their now mutually enriching and nourishing power a wholly new level of joy, energy, creativity, and radical effectiveness. There is a vastly transformative secret hidden in this conscious interweaving of the different expressions of the force of passion. If I had to put it into words, knowing the inadequacy of language to describe such a mystery, I would say this: when our ego becomes the loving servant of the self, when heart, mind, soul, and body are married in the fire of divine passion, a new Person is born. The actions that overflow in peace and joy from such a Person are embued with divine power and divine blessing and can effect miraculous transformations in seemingly hopeless and intractable situations. On millions of us living out the truth of this mystery fearlessly depends the future of the world.

Section 2

The Six Keys of Heart-Centered Living and Evolutionary Relationship Building

Overview of the Six Keys
—Chris Saade

Out of my experience working with couples and meditation on the nature of relationship, I believe there are six keys that help deeply nurture and effectively maintain a relationship—one that is passionate and engaged toward the world. These were set forth in my introduction, but to recap:

I.
Honor and champion the authentic nature of your unique self and the authentic nature of the unique self of others.

II.
Honor and champion the paradoxes of joy and grief, success and defeats, gain and loss.

III.
Honor and champion the deepest desires of your heart and the deepest desires of the heart of others.

IV.
Honor and champion others in their idiosyncratic spirit and advocate their differences.

V.
Co-create an inclusive vision of peace and justice with others that joins your essence with theirs.

VI.
Passionately celebrate the process of co-creation and the journey toward authenticity and solidarity.

Chapter 3
Honor Individual Authenticity

Authenticity
—Chris Saade

The first key is authenticity. Individual authenticity is crucial. Authenticity is tremendously important to allow love to flower and come to its full passionate expression of romance and engagement in the world. Every person has a unique, authentic nature. We have to respect it and support its flowering, and definitely not shame it or pathologize it.

Each person's authenticity is sacred. It is the wellspring of their greatest ability to love. It is about affirming the authenticity of each person, their heart, their body, their mind, and their nature.

In this exploration of authenticity, I would like to cover four themes. The first is particularity, the particularity of each spirit. Second is depth, how spirit lives in our depth. Third is sacred vulnerability. And fourth is genuine respect for authenticity.

Let's start with particularity. The spirit of every individual has an undeniable particularity and a specific authentic orientation. We all share in the spirit of the Divine. We all share in the spirit of life, but that spirit, embodied in us individually, has a unique particularity.

Particularity is extremely important because the unique particularity of your spirit, the idiosyncrasies of your spirit, are the source of the best genius of your spirit—the genius through which you can love others and love the world. Particularity is sacred. The authenticity of your spirit is where and how the incarnation of the Holy Spirit happens in you. It is vitally important to understand and respect the process of becoming who you are, because your (profound) authenticity is an incarnation of the Divine. Incarnation is happening through your unique way of being in the world. You incarnate the way the divine energy walks, talks, and acts, as uniquely you. So it is with your partner. This shifts the dialogue away from how can we change each other to how can we respect each other's essential authenticity and hold it up as a gift of love and passion for the world.

The second point is depth. Authenticity cannot be discovered only at the surface of your being. It needs a deeper descent into the unique truth of who you are. Authenticity is much deeper than just the superficial layers of one's being. An evolutionary love, an evolutionary relationship, will create a space for a lifelong exploration of the depth of the authentic spirit of each individual. In a sense, a relationship of love is a temple of authenticity; two people are in that temple and they look at each other as unique emanations of the Divine.

We cannot emphasize enough that the emanations

of the Divine manifest in specific idiosyncratic spirits. When the temple of love and authenticity expands and a partner is an addition to that temple, and if children are to come into that temple, they too will be emanations of a particular aspect of the spirit of the Divine. All we can do is see our own authentic nature and our partner's authentic nature as sacred, and stand in front of it in awe and reverence. This is a far cry from all the psychoanalyzing of each other that, unfortunately, couples do.

There is also, and very importantly, the global dimension of our authenticity. Our psyche is not a personalized fortress. We live in the world and the world lives in us. We inhabit the Earth and the Earth inhabits us. So in exploring the depths of authentic spirit in one another, we have to ask: "What is the suffering of the world that you and I carry in our spirits? Is it the children of war and poverty? Is it abused animals? Is it the oppression of women? Is it the exploitation of others because of race or culture? Is it the devastation of the environment? What collective longings, hopes and aspirations do we carry?" These collective pulls and memories are a very important and vital part of our humanity.

We all carry the whole suffering and hopes of the world in us, but our spirit will have a definite particular memory and a specific task to fulfill in the world. Andrew says our greatest heartbreak is where our greatest passion emerges. So we have to know our own particular heartbreaks. Then we get a sense of what our spirit is specifically about in the world.

Through the in-depth exploration of our authenticity we ask: "Who are the ancestors who are speaking through me?" My spirit was not born in an empty space; I am not a *tabula rasa*, a blank slate. My spirit came as a continuation of billions of years of history. Ancestors live in me; their dreams, their prayers, their longing, their aspirations, their heroic deeds for justice and peace live in my spirit. All that universal richness lives in my spirit and your spirit.

Then the question is: Who are these ancestors and what are they saying about loving the world, serving the world, transforming the world? Finding the answer requires that you turn your eyes and ears inward and really listen to your authentic spirit and let your spirit, in its own particular form, open up. What you will hear is your own authentic and unique destiny. The way you, as particularly you, serve love. When you do this, you unleash the incredible power of the ancestors, whose longing is in you. You unleash an incredible level of compassion and love. You become the spirit of love for your partner. And it all comes from the world that lives within you. When you awaken that inner world of love and compassion, it gives you the love and compassion to give to the outer world—to your grandchildren, to your beloved partner, to the animals, to all you meet, and to the Earth itself.

Only through our authenticity can we embody the love of the Divine. If we are not truthful about who we are, if we have not surrendered to our own nature and accepted our true self, the love of the Divine cannot embody in us. We block our authenticity, and thus we mitigate the divine soul-print in our personality—our real self.

I am not somebody else. I tremendously respect Andrew Harvey, and I have a great love for him, but I'm not him. I have to carry my own emanation of the Divine, so do you, and so does everybody else.

The third important point regarding authenticity is sacred vulnerability. The quest for authenticity involves the acknowledgment of what we lack, our weaknesses, and the shadows that we bring to a relationship. I know my spirit has great gifts. I also know that my spirit has great lacks—there are no gifts without lacks. There is a lot that I cannot bring to others. I have to be authentic about acknowledging my weaknesses as well as my strengths, because they stand in a paradoxical relationship.

I also have to be authentic about the shadows in me, the uncouth and discourteous behaviors of parts of me. Although these parts are very authentic to me, their expression might still be inelegant. I cannot fully rid myself of these shadows, but I can be conscious, open, and transparent about them. Great passion is never forged in perfection. The quest for perfection, outside of mechanics, is an obsession. Excellence on the other hand is very spiritual and involves mistakes and lacks. Passion develops in transparent vulnerability and the respect we have for our partner's vulnerability, partners who are also attempting to unleash their love to the world and to us.

Vulnerability is part of greatness, part of genius, part of truthful authenticity, and therefore part of love. An authentic relationship is one that has sacred experiences of joy, ecstasy, as well as grief, and defeats, with nothing to hide. It is all part of the glorious journey of a love that is evolving and attempting to unfold.

This leads to the fourth point: the quest for respect. Respect is fundamental for the continuance of love and the feeding of passion. The authenticity of the spirit is sacred. An evolutionary relationship will uphold and support that authenticity of spirit. The old paradigm was: How can I change you (in this isolated, privatized relationship) so we can make it work? However, what we seek in an evolutionary relationship is the sharing of passionate love in service to the world and one another, not changing the authenticity of the other. We seek to support the other in embodying their unique authenticity and taking it to the edge of its creative truth, unique idiosyncrasy, and passion. Our quest becomes one for love and passion, based on respect, not an attempt to transform the other. It is crucial for all of us to learn to deeply respect what is very authentically different from us. We have to train our eyes to see the beauty in the authentic traits of our partner—and seeing that beauty, to respect it. Respect needs to be reconnected to the authentic rather than to the similar or to what we, in our own personal logic, consider correct. It is the authentic that is beautiful, and therefore that deserves our respect.

Exploring the Five Kinds of Authenticity
—Andrew Harvey

R adical authenticity is at the core of the great adventure into a love that transforms your body, heart, mind, and soul. Without that constant quest for an ever deeper, ever more profound, ever richer authenticity, the Divine cannot take both people to a wholly new level of focus, purpose, passion, energy, and truth. In my own quest to find an evolutionary partner, which has taken me into luminous and dark waters, I have found that there really are five kinds of authenticity we need to cultivate at the deepest level if we are going to have a chance, a ghost of a chance, of having the kind of profound transformation that evolutionary love is calling us to.

The first authenticity is this: to get with the evolutionary program of an evolutionary god and evaluate the ways mystical systems and religions have degraded and denied the feminine, have made a static vision of transcendence the goal, instead of a full immersion in a creative god. It is necessary to look at how that has divided the world and begin the sacred practices, reading, the deep study, and the profound meditation and prayer that can help initiate us into the truths the great evolutionary mystics are telling us, which show us that the Universe is God becoming and humanity is an unfinished adventure. It is important to understand this from the depths of one's soul, otherwise one will never plunge deeply enough into the process, or may believe your journey is "finished" when, in fact, the transformations that are possible through the grace of divine love are endless.

The second form of authenticity, and this is crucial in our time, is that both beings who are pursuing this kind of evolutionary love need to get absolutely clear that they are pursuing it at a time in which the world itself is going through a massive global dark night, which is the prelude, potentially, to the birth of a divine embodied humanity. If you are hiding from the intensity, pain, and heartbreak of this global dark night, or if you're in denial, dread, disillusion, or trapped in some fantasy, you will never give yourself to the adventure of evolutionary love because you will not know how essential it is, and how it can give you the kind of fuel we're talking about to go out and really make a sacred difference, to become a midwife of the birth of a new humanity. You have to be able to suffer this crisis at a primordial depth with your partner in a way that doesn't paralyze you, but drives you deeper and deeper into the fiery arms of an all-transforming love.

The third kind of authenticity that is really important for two beings taking this tremendous adventure is this: you must have, at the very least, a commitment to right livelihood, lived authentically. There are many people who are doing good deeds, but they are doing good in a safe way, a way in which they do not actually expose themselves to the suffering of the world or test their whole being in a constant deepening commitment to give everything to the service of the planet. Authentic right livelihood is rare in this world, but when you see a glimpse of it, possibly even in yourself, you must dedicate yourself to a form of service that really absorbs your deepest gifts. And your partner needs to be involved either with you or act separately. Otherwise, the great ideal of evolutionary love, the ideal that an evolutionary love can co-create with the Divine a wholly new world and provide the kind of ecstasy, fuel, energy, passion, and truth for this great transformation cannot be realized. Unless the two people involved in the relationship have an equal commitment to really pouring themselves out in right livelihood, they are in tremendous danger of using their relationship as an addictive drug, which is unfortunately what a great many tantric practitioners do. They use the pursuit of ecstatic relationship as a way of escape, to avoid deep plunging into the world. This is a subtle, but lethal, form of narcissism and aborts the evolutionary impulse.

The fourth authenticity that I have uncovered in myself and in the people I have established this kind of sacred evolutionary relationship with, is that we must be authentic about our need for an all-transforming love.

There are two dangerous things we do in life. The first is to admit how much we love God, long for God, and how much the deepest longing in our whole being is to be one with the Universe in conscious, sober ecstasy. As Rumi says, once you let that longing out, it "burns down your house" and shows you how limited all the other longings are. The second longing is to be brave enough to admit how deeply you long for a transformative human love. To be brave enough to admit how much you need that, you have to be able to admit how vulnerable you are, how lonely you are, how hungry you are for this fulfillment. If you can't do that you will never find the kind of generosity, abandon, and commitment that you are going to need to take this journey with another person. Evolutionary love takes place between two beings who are grounded in their transcendent nature, but who are also absolutely naked and honest about their need for sacred, ecstatic communion with another being. This is dangerous because, as we all know, we can fail. We can believe that someone is our evolutionary partner and they turn out to be a psychopath or a narcissist and we are left flayed and broken in an empty room screaming at the moon. This is dangerous territory, which is why it is so important to approach each step as clearly and completely as possible. Only then can people have the kind of lucidity that will help them choose wisely.

The fifth authenticity is something that Chris spoke about so beautifully. If we are not aware of the deep, sabotaging shadows that all of us have, then the adventure of evolutionary love will be undermined, and we will find that the great love that we are looking for is being resisted by a whole part of us that we've never made conscious or haven't done the work to transmute. To plunge into the great adventure of evolutionary love requires the deepest understanding of how much of us resists this demanding love, how we've inherited the body shame, the pain of a whole civilization as well as our own.

The adventure of evolutionary love is dangerous for another reason: It exposes you to yourself. It reveals to you that for all of your mouthing of sacred truths and your desire for passion and unity and commitment, there is a whole part of you that is lazy, slothful, in denial, corrupt, and profoundly narcissistic. This is shocking, but it is essential to encounter this part of yourself, because you will be dealing with it in ever subtler forms as the transforming process grows more and more intense.

If you root yourself in these five authenticities and work toward them, and your partner does the same, then there is a tremendous chance that love's divine alchemy will turn you to gold.

The Spiritual Component of Authenticity
—A Dialogue between Chris Saade and Andrew Harvey

Chris Saade: This key of authenticity is tremendously important. In the 1600s, the mystic, poet, and priest Angelus Silesius wrote, "The rose is without 'why'; it blooms simply because it blooms." (Previously, in the 14th century, Meister Eckhart taught on that same theme.) A spirit does not come to the world empty, as an empty page upon which society can write or psychologists can manipulate, and so on. A spirit comes with the specificity of being a rose, or being a small bird, or being a large eagle, or being an elephant, or being a running horse. We are born with a specific nature, an authenticity of personality, gifts and lacks. We either develop what are our givens, or we don't, but we cannot deny or change their existence. It is so essential to bow down in respect to that authenticity.

Andrew Harvey: What you're saying is a revolution. There's a wonderful Jewish story which illustrates this beautifully. A rabbi—let's call him Jacob—gets to Heaven and is asked, "What have you loved in your life?" Jacob replies, "Oh! I've loved Abraham, I've loved Moses." And the Divine says to the rabbi, "Jacob, you weren't meant to be Abraham or Moses, you were meant to be Jacob. Go back! Do it again!" For this realization to get through to the human race, two essential revelations have to be given. The first is the core secret of evolutionary mysticism: We are here, not to vanish into the Absolute, as the Eastern traditions have tended to claim, nor to be completely material about our lives, as the Western traditions have increasingly celebrated. We are here to marry the paradox of being grounded in a formless, transcendent truth and light while cultivating our unique self and bringing that unique self to its fullest flowering. This is a vision that is only just starting to break upon the world.

Marry the passion you discover when you reclaim and embody your unique self to the passion to serve the birth of a new humanity and you will be borne into a new level of power, energy, and effectiveness. Imagine what could be accomplished by two people loving and encouraging each other to live this most potent of marriages.

One of the major shadows we must look at is what we call the Golden Shadow. We have been taught by our religious leaders—whether they're Muslim, or Buddhist, or Christian, or whatever—to project our own divinity onto the Prophet Muhammad or onto Jesus or onto Buddha. This has led to a deep self-shaming. We have to take the Golden Shadow back and recognize that everything that we see in Jesus, or in the Prophet, or in the Buddha, lives in us to be claimed or enacted in our own unique way. As Jesus says in Logion 3 of the Gospel of Thomas, "When you know yourselves... then you will know that you are children of the Living One. But if you do not know yourselves, you will live in poverty, and you are the poverty." Evolutionary love will not be able to be incubated in the current religious, guru, or New Age systems because it demands that people step outside the religious inhibitions of all of the major systems and claim their divinity and do this radical work of marrying the authentic self, rooted consciously in its light-origin to its mission of sacred service.

Chris Saade: Most people look for a "correct" way of being, a "correct" way of being love. They lose the authenticity of their own spiritual embodiment. Self-shaming is, in a sense, a re-crucifixion of the Divine in us.

Andrew Harvey: Absolutely.

Chris Saade: Because, that spirit, that unique, particular, idiosyncratic spirit that I am carrying which needs to come alive and serve the world, is shamed, because it is not what others are.

It's amazing how many people struggle with this. They can admire Gandhi, they can admire Mother Teresa, but when it comes to their own spirit—their own authentic nature—they succumb to self-shame because their spirit is different from these famous, well-known spiritual figures. The essential part of the transformation we are seeking, this grassroots unleashing of love-in-action, has to come through a profound respect for every individual authenticity and for the sacred task of every individual spirit.

Andrew Harvey: That requires a smashing of the idols. I remember when I was working on the *The Tibetan Book of Living and Dying,* the Dalai Lama said, "Your Buddha nature is as good as the Buddha's Buddha nature." He was being playful, but he was also saying, we must produce a book that reveals to people that everything in the book can be done by them. "Enlightenment" doesn't have to be projected outwards. But very few mystical or religious leaders are really giving that message. The New Age claims to give that message, but then, it defines the authentic life as being peaceful, passive, and gentle, not seeing the negative—all of this nonsense.

Chris Saade: But that's the same problem; it defines authenticity in one way or the other, rather than allowing freedom to sculpt our marvelous diversity of authenticities.

Andrew Harvey: Yes!

Chris Saade: And we cannot define the authenticity of the spirit. It will define itself differently in each individual.

Andrew Harvey: Right!

Chris Saade: Because some spirits embody like a very peaceful bird, and tend to be very meditative, but some spirits come to Earth like a roaring lion and their role is to become that roaring lion, like the bird is to become the bird. In some people, their spirit is to serve thousands and other spirits are to serve one or two people. This is so important because it is about reclaiming the individual Buddhahood, the Christhood, of every particular spirit. Our authenticity is unique, yet it is indivisibly connected to love. We can only fully understand the nature of our own spirit when we dedicate it to service, for the love of the world.

Andrew Harvey: When millions of human beings truly grasp this, we will be able to create together a new world. The patriarchal systems which have privatized the search for enlightenment as well as the search for love speak of liberation as freedom from the world, the body, relationships, and action. But what the God of evolution teaches, the God that is Mother as well as Father, is that liberation is not just this inner freedom from the world but also the wild and transformative freedom to take on the madness of the world, the difficulty of authentic relationship, so as to become instruments of divine love and its plan to divinize matter in the whole of life. What the evolutionary Divine reveals to us is that you cannot discover your true self only in its relationship to eternal being; you must discover it also as a tool of eternal becoming, as Kabir's child dancing on the Father/Mother's burning dance floor, dancing in ever deeper, evermore embracing relationship, and in evermore focused and powerful works of compassion and justice.

Chapter 4
Honor the Paradox of Joy and Grief

Seven Opposites to Explore in Paradox
—Andrew Harvey

Another key to the kind of evolutionary love that we're talking about is paradox. Without a whole-sale commitment to embrace paradox on every level, no evolutionary love is possible—because paradox is the nature of the Universe itself.

The greatest vision that we've been given of God, and this is a vision that is at the core of all of the major mystical traditions, is that God is a coincidence of opposites. God is working as much in destruction as in creation. God is working as much in chaos as in order. God is working as much in agony as in joy. God is working as much in horror as in beauty. It's easy to say those things, but to actually allow yourself to experience the Divine in all the things that are most terrifying to the ego, is the key to entering into the evolutionary fire.

I want to talk about two beings who did this so simply and beautifully. The first is, of course, Rumi, who, upon his awakening, lived in divine human paradox for thirty years. He wrote this wonderful quatrain:

One day in your wine shop, I drank a little wine,
And threw off this robe of my body,
And knew, drunk on you, the world is harmony.
Creation, destruction, I am dancing for them both.

The second is my great teacher and my great heart's beloved, Father Bede Griffiths, who said to me, "We will not become an adult race until we really enter into the paradoxical nature of God and until we can bless God in all the things that we are most terrified of. It's through that gate of acceptance, of oneness as this dance of opposites, that we can enter into the transforming, evolutionary field."

The central image of the new evolutionary lover is the dancer. I love the representation of Shiva that is called, *Shiva Nataraja*, because you see the Divine Beloved dancing and creating the Cosmos out of this dance, holding in one hand the flame of destruction, and in other, the drum of creation. In this image is the kind of dynamic balancing of opposites that you need to discover and embody to become, in your own way, the dancer of your full sacred identity in life. Once you truly begin to accept this at the profoundest level, at the cellular level, there are seven paradoxes you need to be able to dance with.

First, you need to be able to dance with the paradox of your essential nature as an en-souled body and an embodied soul. You must know the needs of your body and the needs of your soul and bring them together, understanding that your soul is embodying yourself as you. Your soul hasn't "fallen" into this material dimension. It has chosen embodiment for a sacred purpose and with great joy. No one has expressed this more precisely than the great Kabbalistic mysti, Moses de Leon:

> *The purpose of the soul entering this body is to display her powers and actions in this world, for she needs an instrument. By descending to this world, she increases the flow of her power to guide the human being through the world. Thereby she perfects herself above and below, attaining a higher state by being fulfilled in all dimensions. If she is not fulfilled both above and below, she is not complete.*
>
> *Before descending to this world, the soul is emanated from the mystery of the highest level. While in this world, she is completed and fulfilled by this lower world. Departing this world, she is filled with the fullness of all the worlds, the world above and the world below.*
>
> *At first, before descending to this world, the soul is imperfect; she is lacking something. By descending to this world, she is perfected in every dimension.*

As an evolutionary lover, the second paradox that you need to be able to dance with is the paradox of peace and passion. You need to be simultaneously grounded in a transcendent peace to find the energy and hope and power and compassion that relieve the stress of the passion needed to fuel the evolution of this relationship.

The third paradox that you will need to be able to endure to create an evolutionary love with another being is the paradox of patience and urgency. If you are not patient with yourself, and if you're not patient with the other, nothing great can be built. If you're too patient, you become codependent and you become too accepting of the shadow in the other or the shadow in yourself. So patience has to be married to a constant urgency borne out of sacred passion to take both people to the next level. How you marry patience and urgency is one of the great secrets of evolution and it can only be done through profound spiritual practice and shadow work.

The fourth paradox of evolutionary love that you must embrace is that of great suffering and ecstasy. The suffering will come from your growing knowledge of your own resistance, shadow wounds, and the ways in which they hurt, not only you, but the other. Because you've chosen this adventure, you will experience the ways in which your habitual forms of acting and thinking, formed out of your trauma, really hurt the other at a very deep level. This will cause you pain. You will need to be strong enough to bear that pain and to work with it humbly. You will also need to cultivate a great strength of your whole being to stand the ecstatic revelation that will come through evolutionary love, because in your practice of it, you will be burst into oneness with the Universe. You will be burst into oneness with every being that suffers. You will see the divine light as you make love to your partner. You will be taken into realms of ecstasy which can be as dangerous as the realms of suffering if you haven't done the work to prepare your whole being to receive their molten energies.

The fifth paradox you need to learn to dance with is the paradox of the "coincidence" of light and the dark, both in the nature of God and in your own divine nature. You will not be able to separate God into pure love and light and demonize the dark. You will have to find the treasures in your shadow, the treasures in failure, the treasures in grief, the treasures in loss, the treasures in abandonment, the treasures in trauma. This requires a radical blessing and embracing of the shadow, which in the end, will shatter your ego and open it up to the higher powers of divine love. This, in my experience, is the most difficult work of all, impossible without the rugged illumined strength that only spiritual practice can build.

As you grow into evolutionary love, the major work becomes shadow work. I am lucky enough to have been given very great experiences of the light, but in the last twenty years I've concentrated on working with my shadow, because being grounded in the light is not enough. It has taken an enormous effort to be able to bless what I'm discovering about my shadow and the shadow of others. But I find that in the effort to bless my own and other shadows, immense new powers of compassion, tenderness, and deep skillful means arise. Without those deep skillful means, you have no hope of negotiating the enormous fragility that an authentic, sacred, evolutionary relationship demands.

The sixth paradox is the need for the solitude in which to cultivate your deepest inner self and the need for rich communion with your partner and with others. If you have too much solitude, your communion gets muddy, and if you have too much communion, you lose connection with the mystery of your authentic self. Rigorously working out your true need for solitude with how best to experience communion with the other, and with your friends, and with the world, is a very holy undertaking. It is very difficult, but it can be done through prayer and meditation and through grounded compassion, both for your own self and its needs for repose and wise self-care and for the pain and needs of others.

The last paradox is one that permeates this path of evolutionary love. How do you dance between sacred privacy and public service? How do you make the time to explore and expand and create a profound and protected sacred privacy with the being you love while always remaining responsive to helping others? How do you balance this sacred privacy with the need to extend yourself in sacred service to the world? This requires a subtle negotiation between partners, and it requires a paradoxical and simultaneous commitment to the intensity, purity, holiness, passion, truth of the relationship, *and* to the fundamental goal of that relationship, which is to become strong enough to really step up to your sacred mission in the world.

The Psychological Paradoxes That Couples Experience
–Chris Saade

Paradox is part of the essence of the nature of reality, including, for many ancient spiritualities, of divine reality. The understanding of paradox is crucial for the unleashing of love. When we work at accepting paradox and integrating paradox, we achieve something that is very special. We achieve becoming at peace—at peace with our sacred humanity and our sacred authentic spirit. It is the understanding of the paradox of life, life with its beauty and great disappointments, that protects us from succumbing to nihilism.

Life itself is a powerful paradox of both peacefulness and passion—joy and grief, wounds and blessings. We grow in love or we come to love life as it is—life in its full paradoxical givens. There is the beautiful story about Jesus who "came to reconcile to himself all things, whether on Earth or in Heaven." He came to reconcile us with our nature, with who we are. When we are not at peace with the paradoxical nature of our being, we are at war with that nature. We expect that we are going to transcend our paradoxical life, and we cannot, so we become deeply aggrieved or in despair. When we are at war with that nature, we are paralyzed and we are depressed and we are battered and we don't have the energy to give to loving the world and loving our partner.

In most psychological and spiritual literature, paradox has been exiled and shunned. Instead, the goal is to achieve total peace, total harmony, total oneness, and total contentment. This puts us into an even greater battle with the reality of who we are on this sacred journey.

In Greek and Phoenician thinking, the number two was essential, and the number two meant paradox. It is said that to be able to walk with the gods and goddesses, you had to understand the meaning of the number two. When you walk with the Divine you will be filled with enthusiasm, but you will also be filled with the grief of the Divine. You will be filled with the power and the inspiration of the Divine as well as the sensitivity of the Divine. The idea of paradox was central to the teaching of the Chinese Tao. It is crucial for the flowering of evolutionary love, to grasp the significance and the power of the paradox.

There are six paradoxes that come up a great deal in the psychological life of a couple. The first one is strength and vulnerability. Most couples have a lot of strength, both individually and as a couple. They also have a lot of vulnerabilities. Individually and as a couple, both strength and vulnerability need to be honored. We must not see strength as the part we respect and vulnerability as the part that is weak. Vulnerability is part of the genius of love, and part of the ability to feel love.

The second paradox within relationship is joy and grief. To get together and celebrate joy is a great gift— but so is the sharing of grief. When grief arises in a relationship, we have to be able to see it as sacred, to actually feel it as a moment of heart, a "participation mystique" in divine grief, a communion with the broken heart of the Divine for our world.

In the Louvre Museum there are incredible paintings depicting grief and people stand before them for hours. They see the beauty and the ecstasy in grief. Through art they understand that grief does not have to be shunned. The paintings tell us we are not to run away from grief, but to realize that joy and grief are in a dance, a continuous circle of mutuality.

Another relationship paradox is breakthroughs and breakdowns. A relationship that worships breakthroughs but is desolate about breakdowns is a relationship that sets its course for the unreal and will lose its passion. Passion flourishes in the real. Passion develops in a ground that is smooth as well as one that is tilled and opened up. Passion flourishes through breakdowns *and* breakthroughs.

This evolutionary journey of love can only be taken through honoring the breakthroughs and breakdowns of the past, the present, and the future. A relationship has to be able to bless both, to honor both its defeats and its successes, and to respect both.

Then there is the paradox of freedom and union, the importance of independence from, and connection with, the other. We need not to be afraid of differentiating from our partner. We need to differentiate and deepen our own sense of authentic individuation. We also need to generously bond and seek those moments we become one with our partner and totally lost in their heart and body. To know that place where we become one and then to be able to go back to moments of total freedom within our own unique spirit. There's so much to this paradox and we will explore it further in the section on evolutionary sexuality. Unfortunately, psychotherapy tends to underline the importance of differentiation while often forgetting the similar crucial importance of the deep bonding of love.

Another paradox, the one of contentment and struggle, keeps us connected to the world. The ability to be content is important yet it has been made almost an idol. We love to see all the sacred images that depict contentment and acceptance, where everything-is-fine-and-all-is-well-forever-and-ever. If there is a struggle in our psyche or a struggle in our relationship, we see it as a failure of either our psychological work or our spiritual work. This kind of mentality, the refusal of the paradox of contentment and struggle, cuts us off from the world itself. It takes us into an idealized and privatized relationship and that's not the reality of the world. The world is made of peace and beauty as well as demanding struggle. It's made of contentment and conflict. We have to realize that as individuals we are a microcosm of the world, and in a relationship we are a microcosm of the world, and the fullness of the truth of the world within us has to be respected.

The last paradox we are considering is confidence and anguish. I know for a fact that so many people who are archetypally able to profoundly sense the difficulty of situations and thus feel anxiety, are shamed by their partners, by their therapists, and by their spiritual teachers. Let us remember that although the power of love does release our highest power, and puts us in communion with the Divine, love also makes us more sensitive and empathetic. Through love we can move mountains and that is a wonderful feeling. But love also opens up our anguish. We are anguished about the possibility of loss. We are anguished about what's happening in the world, about the threat of destruction, about what is happening to the beauty of human culture and how it is being swallowed by exploitation and oppression. We are anguished about how our democracy is besieged by mega money on one hand, and violent demagoguery on the other hand. Anguish is a form of intelligence—so is grief, so is vulnerability, so is strength, and contentment, and peace. This is the essential nature of reality. To be authentic is to carry many paradoxes, it is to be proud of our unceasing laughter and our tears, our moments of elation and our moments of trembling... So we are learning, whether we're looking at philosophical paradoxes or spiritual paradoxes or psychological paradoxes, to welcome them all. We stand in the midst of them—proud, strong, and welcoming.

A relationship that welcomes all of these paradoxes is a relationship that can unleash the passionate love of the Divine and serve the world. It does not have to protect itself from the paradoxes of life. Creating an ongoing privatized island of contentment is impossible. I have not known any relationship that could achieve this for more than a very short period of time.

Couples who pursue the impossible set themselves up to fail. They lose the strength of their spirit and they end up turning their backs to the world. It is an illusion to think that we can achieve a permanent sense of peace and contentment without loosing our heart, our passion, our creativity, and our sense of active solidarity. By honoring the paradox, and the partial place of peace and contentment within that paradox, we honor life, we honor ourselves as proud humans, and we honor our human (and paradoxical relationships). Because it's all one. We are all one. The world is struggling, so am I, so is my relationship, so is my family, so is my body, so is everything. There is dignity in the struggle undertaken with mindfulness and serenity.

We are filled with hope, filled with beauty, filled with enthusiasm, filled with Eros, filled with energy and vitality. We are also blessed with wounds and weaknesses and trembling. We are called to love wholeheartedly, to love the Earth, to love the real, to love the real in ourselves, in others, and in the world. Thus we come to be in communion with what is really true with every tear and every smile, with every show of strength and every moment of trembling vulnerability. It is out of this love for the fullness of life that real transformation happens. It is out of this love that we can truly respect our relationships in their beauty and challenges.

The Paradox of Evolutionary Love
—A Dialogue between Andrew Harvey and Chris Saade

Andrew Harvey: The last thing we want to do is give the impression of evolutionary love as another New Age denial of the dark, or another purely heroic struggle. So much of the true nature of evolutionary love becomes evident in failure, in sadness, in loss, in vulnerability. This is the supreme paradox of evolution, which we really need to attend to: The greatest light is born out of the greatest darkness.

This is the paradox that we are living at this moment. As evolutionary partners, we cannot afford not to know that greatest darkness in the world, and in ourselves. This means radical confrontation with the unprecedented shadows of this unprecedented crisis. Both partners in an evolutionary love journey will be bombarded by the psychic free radicals of disbelief that the crisis could be so immense. To deny that the crisis is so immense is to threaten the whole of humanity and the planet itself. It exhibits a profound death wish not to be here, a profound hunger not to be here.

If two people take this evolutionary love adventure without knowing that their psyches are being bombarded at an unprecedented intensity by these communal shadows arising out of this devastating global dark night, they will not be able to tend each other's being in the way that they will need to tend it.

We must all become aware of the shadows that we ourselves have that cause us to collude with these global shadows and keep them alive. We must all become aware of the ways in which we have been trained as narcissists in this culture, a culture that adores and rewards narcissism on every level. We must become aware of how dangerous this lethal self-love is. We must become aware that we've been taught to be slaves of comfort and to be afraid of losing comfort. We must become aware that we have been trained to be terrified of being our true selves because everybody knows that being your true self can provoke tremendous distress and rage and antagonism. If we are not aware we're terrified of standing up and standing out, we will never be able to inspire ourselves to grow more courageous.

Chris Saade: Being aware! Being mindful of our true and unique individual authenticity! The great gift of feminist psychology and feminist theology is that it has shown us how oppression turns us against our body, our psyche, our authenticity, our emotions, and our heart. This is the real oppression. We see this in abusive families when abused individuals most often hate the reality of their body, and hate the reality of their humanity because their body and/or their humanity was rejected and shamed.

When we come to accept the truth that we are heroic beings with wounds, that we walk the heroic journey of the heart with our lacks and with our vulnerabilities, then we are able to love the real. We are able to see the magnificence of the person that walks beside us. He or she is trying within their means to bring that New Jerusalem on Earth, the day when the lamb and the lion will sit together in peace. We come to greatly respect our partner who is, though imperfectly, attempting to affirm greater freedom, peace, and justice in the world. That perception of the other as an activist of love will allow our loving respect to become the foreground of our relationship. This will allow us to love our partner in their authentic and so beautifully human reality.

Andrew Harvey: Right. And real compassion can be born.

Chris Saade: Great compassion! Then we come to our partner who is also lame and flawed, like ourselves, and we see the magnificence in the lame and the flawed, and then fall in love with their humanity again and again. Unless we do this with the understanding that the greatest light comes out of the greatest dark, we cannot love life in the world, in the planet, and in ourselves.

Andrew Harvey: How can we possibly take an evolutionary adventure into divine love without realizing that we're doing it in a world exploding with potential destruction and all kinds of unprecedented problems and shadows? It would be like walking into a forest fire dressed in a paper tutu. It can't be done.

Chris Saade: And the effect of these problems is also constantly exploding in our own psyche.

Andrew Harvey: Yes, exploding in us at all moments whether we realize it or not. There is no way out of this awareness. And thank God! This awareness gives us a much deeper level of compassion for ourself and our partner. Instead of using our partner as a narcissistic love object to project back to us some perfect version of ourself, we expose ourself in both our glory and our dereliction.

Chris Saade: That is the real hero.

Andrew Harvey: Right!

Chris Saade: If you look at the ancient Phoenician and Greek heroes, they were never perfect heroes. They were heroes with weaknesses, with vulnerabilities.

Andrew Harvey: Right, but they aren't the kind of heroes that we celebrate in our power crazy culture. As the evolutionary adventure of love progresses, we will need great sober prudence, tremendous sober awareness. That can only be born out of our knowledge of our own shadow and the shadow of the partner, and the shadow of the world.

Chris Saade: That's the wisdom of the paradox. There's another paradox we haven't talked about yet, the paradox of anger and peace. Anger and peace are not opposite to each other as pop spirituality teaches. Anger is such a reviled emotion. But it's actually a sacred and necessary emotion. If we take the energy of anger and, instead of destroying and reviling others, we channel it to bless, to love, and to create justice, it's an energy that then becomes a harbinger of peace—but to do so we have to feel and know our anger. As we go into the journey of love, there will be moments where we will experience anger at what is deeply hurting us. Listening to the signals and wisdom offered by one's anger does not negate inner peace. Anger that is repressed will eventually shatter peace. Anger that is not intentionally and creatively channeled will be destructive. However, anger that is not dumped on the other, rather listened to inwardly, can become a source of deep knowing, a guide toward deeper levels of our own authenticity, and a blessing to self and partner. We need to learn to master the energy of anger, as an expert horse rider masters her skills in guiding powerful horses. To do so we have to first honor our feelings of anger, like a seasoned rider honors his horse- to welcome intentional anger (not abuse of course) as part of the healthy life paradox of peace and anger.

Andrew Harvey: We also experience anger at our partner for not being with us or not knowing what we're feeling.

Chris Saade: Exactly. The relationship that is evolutionary and willing to be passionate creates the space for intentional anger. It does not accept a destructive expression of anger, but it accepts that the anger is there. An evolutionary relationship is committed to and engaged in bringing love, justice, and transformation to the world. Therefore, these emotions of sadness, anger, and anguish must become dedicated to serve life and love rather than be used in a privatized and destructive way. All authentic feelings are important—a window into the truth of life. However, we need to learn to express them with love and through love.

Andrew Harvey: If we aren't aware of these communal challenges, at the deepest and fundamental level, we will never evolve the skillful means that enable us to work with our grief, our pain, and our outrage and transmute them into the fierce compassion energy that can fuel our service.

Chris Saade: When those emotions arrive in me, great grief, vulnerability, anger, or anxiety—let me transmute these (not block or denigrate) into a loving expression, into loving social action, into a longing for justice. But there is also another voice, one that is introjected in me, a remnant of oppressive ideation, that says, "Let me take your anger and your anxiety and make out of it a moment of victimization and aggression." That is a slippery path that could easily lead into control or abuse.

I have to be aware of these two voices in myself, totally aware. Otherwise, I'll be abducted again and again.

Andrew Harvey: Otherwise we don't know the difference between our divine anger and our neurotic traumatized anger.

Chris Saade: All grief emerges as an authentic expression of life, and an intelligent response to events, but its expression can becomes abducted into self-victimization or into abuse of others.

Andrew Harvey: This is why the skillful means acquired from this radical shadow work is essential. Without these spiritual skillful means, the expression of what could potentially be divine becomes privatized, neurotic, and the source of abuse as well as a subtle, deadly self destruction.

Chapter 5
Honor the Heart

The Four Aspects of the Heart
—Chris Saade

The third key for nurturing and sustaining a passionate and socially engaged relationship has to do with the heart, with honoring and respecting the heart, and in making the heart a priority–not only for the individuals involved, but also for the relationship itself.

In older traditions, the Divine is called the "Heart of hearts." Our heart abides in the heart of the Divine. Similarly, the heart of the Divine resides within our heart. Through the heart we have an intimate and direct connection with the Divine, the Source of life—with the vibrancy of life and love. To explore the heart, we will look at four of its primary aspects: the deep feelings of the heart, the longings of the heart, the desires of the heart, and the calling of the heart.

Let us start with the deep feelings of the heart. The heart is not about sentimentality, emotionality, and reactive feelings. It is about something much deeper in us that we recognize intuitively. It is about our deep feelings, longings, and desires. As individuals, we know when we touch a place that belongs to the infinite, and yet resides in us as finite beings. It is in our heart that we find feelings of amazing compassion for all the children of the world, as well as for the animals, the Earth, and for all those who suffer, are mistreated, and are oppressed. We discover that those feelings alive within our heart are unbounded. It is the Divine within our heart that holds an immense capacity for compassion for all and for everything. By allowing ourselves to feel deeply, we uncover a dimension that is rich in wisdom and luminosity.

Through the heart we also discover the ability, day after day, to fall in love, yet again, with this difficult journey called life. In our heart we discover the ability to see life, the journey, the struggle, and the epic adventure with the eyes of the lover. We do this with eyes that are inspired, touched, excited, and are in awe of the beauty within life. Just as we fall in love with the beautiful in the world and in the Earth, we also fall in love, day after day, with our partner in our relationship.

That ability to fall in love is one of the great mysteries of life. When you think about the vast difficulties we experience within our lives: relationships, sickness, death, poverty, unemployment, ecological violation, etc. – it is a great miracle that we have not all become obsessively cynical and despondent. But there is something in our hearts that can feel the joy, the possibility, and the hope of the world even when we are challenged.

Stefane Hessel was a French diplomat of Jewish origin. In his nineties he was shaking the minds and hearts of France with his speech and his books, calling us to get engaged and to fall in love again with the world and the Earth. He called on us to become advocates for our besieged democracies as well as ecological activists. Hessel was a man who knew suffering. He was imprisoned in a concentration camp during the Second World War. He then joined the Resistance. Eventually he worked with Eleanor Roosevelt to write the Declaration of Human Rights. I have been very impacted by Hessel's call to serve as a falling in love with a cause. Even throughout his 90s, he kept championing the idea that the greatest gift a human can receive is to fall passionately in love with another, and with a cause. To him, falling in love is the greatest gift.

Now let us discuss the deep longings of the heart. The deeper we go into these longings, the more we discover their power–the more we learn to honor them. We come to know that they are the longings of the world itself, the world longing for justice and peace, as well as for reconciliation and inclusion. We also discover that our profound longings belong to the world. The Divine longs within us. Our ancestors long within us. We discover, through our deep longing, that the children of the world who are oppressed and abused pray through us. We discover that the howling of animals who are being decimated is heard within our longing. It is so important in an evolutionary relationship to create the space where that longing is given voice, is respected, and is not psychoanalyzed and regarded as some form of aberration or pathological discontent. An evolutionary relationship will encourage each person in the relationship to bring out that longing–to speak its force and power, to have its depths heard, and to also be creatively guided by it.

In the heart, we also discover our desires to create. Not the wish for fame but "When I look within, in my deepest recesses, what does my heart long to create?" Usually, the first response of a lot of people I work with is, "I don't know." So, we need to take the time to listen to the heart. Just listen. And then ask the question; "What is it that I authentically desire to do to make a difference in the world?" People find that within their heart there is a particular and generous desire to serve. Not scripted by someone else, but rather sprouting from their own authenticity: "I desire to go back to school to study and then write a thesis about ecological issues;" "I desire to join a humanitarian organization;" "I desire to get people to get together in my corporation to create a fund for community work." The desires that come through the heart are amazing. These are the desires of the Divine itself flowing through our hearts. If we repress the heart and thereby repress these desires, we are neutralizing and numbing the divine love pouring through us.

In an evolutionary relationship it is essential to ask this simple question of desire. Once per week, sit with your beloved on the veranda, outside in a garden, or in your favorite place in the house. Look into the eyes of your partner and ask, "What do you want to create? What are the desires of your heart?" Listen to your partner's response. Listen as though you are listening to a sacred song. Allow yourself to be inspired and to support your partner in the pursuit of their heart's desire.

Every person has a particular calling to serve the world. We are called upon to do something, not a hundred things. We are not called to transform everything. However, there is one thing (or maybe two) upon which we are called to make a big difference in the world. If we listen, that calling will draw the path of our destiny. It will open the doors of our creativity and unleash our love. If we remain faithful to that calling, we will know it as sacred, and as something to hold with the greatest of love and respect.

Every relationship has its ultimate temple in the temple of the heart. In every home, there needs to be an altar for the heart. It could be an altar that you actually create or a symbolic one. It is a special space in which both hearts of the couple are heard with no analysis, no shaming or putting down, and no rationalization. Instead, both partners simply listen, recognizing that they are listening to something very sacred. Open yourselves to receive the revelation of your hearts. From this revelation, you then act.

This is what mystical traditions have taught us. That is what spiritual psychology is all about. If we consistently analyze our desires and our callings, there is a danger of killing the luminous presence of the Divine because this calling *is* a mystery. A desire is not only a sacred mystery, but also a longing. It is ultimately a visitation from the Divine.

An evolutionary relationship that holds the heart with a deep respect, and knows this profound connection between one's heart and the heart of the Divine, will continuously gather the powers of love. It is like inviting a river of energy into your home. It will course through your home and propel you out into the world. Once you allow the unleashing of desires and the calling of the heart, you will find yourself looking toward the world to make your mark as an individual and as a couple. If you listen and follow, you find yourself greatly blessed by the heart and by the presence of sacred love. Your hands become the hands of love-in-action, reaching out with the energy of a heart burning with compassion and solidarity.

Connecting the Heart with the Sacred Heart
—Andrew Harvey

I want to plunge into the mystical vision of the heart because the heart we are talking about isn't the physical heart and it isn't the way in which the heart is usually talked about as a fountain of emotion.

The mystics of every tradition recognize that there is a center on the psycho-spiritual body that is a slightly towards the right of the center of the chest. That center, which the Sufis called "the royal center," which the Hindus call the *anahata*, and which the Christian mystics call the "sacred heart," is the crucial center to open on the path to transformation. This heart center enshrines, as its ultimate secret, a spark of divine consciousness, which reveals to you your non-dual identity with the great bliss consciousness that is creating the Universe. What happens when the heart center opens fully is that you see reality, as Rumi says, "with reality's own eyes." As another Sufi mystic Tirmidhi wrote,

"When the heart is polished and luminous, it sees the kingdom of divine glory and the divine glory becomes naked to it." To have this experience and then to put its revelation of all created love into action is why we are here.

Another essential insight that the great evolutionary mystics have about this heart center is that it is, through a mystery of grace, the marriage bed in which the sacred marriage takes place, the sacred marriage between masculine and feminine, between light energy and physical matter, between light and dark, between all the paradoxes that dance in us in our action in the world.

So the heart isn't only an organ of insight into divine reality. It is also the alchemical crucible where our evolution is worked out, where the marriage of the body to the soul is worked out, where the marriage of the feminine sides of your personality to the masculine side is worked out, where the marriage of all the paradoxes is worked out. This is the core passion of evolutionary love—to open the heart center and to keep it open through adoration, gratitude, praise, and surrender so this sacred marriage of opposites can, in that center, be realized and consummated.

Here is an image of how this works. The physical heart pumps blood around the whole body. Without the physical heart pumping the body wouldn't be healthy, and if anything happens to that mechanism, we die. On the higher levels of evolution, the spiritual heart plays exactly the same role. It pumps the energy of the light, the *shakti* of the light, through and around all the spiritual centers so the whole of your spiritual body becomes unified. This is your *sahasrara* chakra, the chakra that is open to the transcendent, your third eye, your heart center, your throat center, the Hara, the sex center, the base chakra—all seven of them align and unify into a golden column of power at the center of your being, which is constantly fed by the fires erupting out of the open sacred heart.

This is not just an ecstatic experience, and not just a holy mystery, it is the key to evolution. The evolution of the divine human depends upon the descent of divine light into the heart center which then pumps the glory, the power, the passion, the peace, the energy of that light all around your being to transfigure it.

The core truth of the sacred heart is that it is always in connection with the Divine. When you get into connection with it, you discover that incessant connection which is the greatest source of peace, energy, confidence and courage, all of which grow more luminous and grounded as the evolutionary transformation proceeds. To discover, celebrate, and sustain this most intimate of connections is essential then to support your power to love at the full stretch that you need to love. Nobody has ever expressed this intimate connection of the heart with God more sublimely than Rumi.

In his *Table Talk* he says, "In every circumstance or situation, the heart is drunk on the Beloved, occupied only with adoration of Him. The heart has no need to travel the various stages of the path. It is the place. It is the placeless place where He lives already, and the love it loves Him with is a spark of the fire of His own passion. There is a rope of light between your heart and His that nothing can weaken or break, and it is always in His hands. The heart never needs to fear ambush from bandits. The heart does not need a horse and saddle and provisions and a complicated map. It is the body that needs and is chained to these things. Wherever you may be, in whatever situation or circumstance you may find yourself, strive always to be a lover, and a passionate lover. Once you possess your heart in love, you will always be a lover. In the tomb, at the resurrection, and in paradise forever and ever."

Before we can be a lover of another human being with total intensity and truth we have to awaken the heart in this essential primordial relation with the sacred heart of the Universe, and we have to keep it open through mantra, through prayer, through inspiration, through adoration. This is the key work for us to do both separately and together in the new evolutionary relationship.

When open, the heart center reveals three interrelated things. It reveals the Divine Light as the essence of every created thing, as the fundamental creative agent appearing in and as everything. It reveals that the Divine Light lives in you as your essential consciousness. And—this is crucial and often ignored—it reveals that as someone who is being given the original blessing of divine consciousness in the core of your heart center, you have something of the responsibility of God, something of the noble, glorious responsibility of God to protect and safeguard this creation that you now recognize as entirely saturated with divine beauty, presence, and light. It cannot be, and must not be, a private experience.

You have not had an authentic experience of the sacred heart unless it drives you into the arms of service to do whatever you can with your unique gifts to heal the agony of the world, to stand up for the voiceless, to stand up for the oppressed. Don't talk to me about how you've had the revelation of the heart if you haven't plunged into service, because I will know that you're faking it. Maybe unconsciously, but you're faking it. It is not yet real. The heart has to get bloody in reality, just as God gets bloody in reality, otherwise it's not a divine experience.

Don't go anywhere near the heart if you're not prepared to suffer, if you're not prepared to accept your portion of the heartbreak of God. This is why people are terrified of the authentic heart. They love it when you talk about the heart in a soft sentimental way, about how we're here just to spread sweetness and light. That is, of course, true, but it is only one part of the truth of the heart.

One of the great revelations of the Sufi mystical traditions which is repeated again and again by Rumi and all the Sufi mystics is this: When you approach the heart, the real heart, what you're given in the end—not in the beginning because you couldn't stand it—what you're given in the end is an initiation into the vast heartbreak of God at the appalling cruelty and madness of what we've done to the world.

There is a great text by a ninth century Sufi, Hayunnah, that describes with scientific precision the ascending stages of the journey of the sacred heart:

> *Whoever loves God will win his friendship.*
> *Whoever becomes joyful will fill with passion.*
> *Whoever is full of passion will become amazed.*
> *Whoever becomes amazed will become brave.*
> *Whoever becomes brave will reach Him.*
> *Whoever reaches Him will enter into union.*
> *Whoever enters into union will become a knower.*
> *Whoever becomes a knower will be drawn near.*
> *Whoever draws near will never fall asleep.*
> *And the rays of sublime heartbreak will engulf him.*

Hayunnah reveals in those glorious last two lines, that the consummation of the work in the heart is to become strong and surrendered enough to be engulfed by "rays of sublime heartbreak," so we can bear our own unique portion of the heartbreak of God. We are called to be so infused by that "sublime heartbreak" that our entire being and the actions that flow from us are a fire with passionate compassion. Dare to imagine for a moment the cosmic depth of the heartbreak of the Mother at all the ways humanity has betrayed, degraded and desecrated the relationship she has offered it, the depth of the agony of the divine heart at the horrifying destruction that is now threatening the future of humanity and a great deal of nature. An authentic evolutionary lover will be taken into an experience of this cosmic anguish of God—an experience that will transform him or her into someone willing to gamble his or her whole life away for the divine desire to see humanity healed and liberated from the inner demons now destroying its soul and endangering its life and the lives of billions of other creatures.

It is almost impossible in a world dominated by devastating narcissistic forms of power to imagine a relationship that does not use and thrive on illegitimate uses of power. The only way in which you can ever have an evolutionary relationship is to give up power, to give up any kind of power of the ego that you have over the other person. You can only do this if you are so in love with the sanctity of the sacred heart of the other that any violation of that heart—by your shadow, your use of power, your need to be right, your need to establish your version of things over the other—is seen not just as an unfortunate human defect, but as a kind of rape of the soul.

You cannot evolve a sacred relationship without truly, in the name of the heart, committing to ash all your conscious and unconscious drives to power. It's only when you see just how driven by power you are that you realize how much work there is to be done. When you really take that work on, the purest and most powerful part of your heart will be released. Only then will you truly be a guardian and a protector of the heart of the one you love, and the co-creator of a unit of sacred relationship in which you will experience directly the mystery and blessing of what Jesus meant when he said, speaking out of the truth of the divine heart. "When two or three are gathered in my name, I will be there."

The Necessity of Trusting the Heart
—A Dialogue between Chris Saade and Andrew Harvey

Chris Saade: How can love truly happen if we do not allow the heart to be open? One thing that I have seen consistently throughout my work with people in our workshops is that we are brainwashed to not trust the heart and to not believe in the heart. We think that the heart is somehow soiled and that what comes from within is somehow irrational or unacceptable. In privatized emotionality, we experience the heart at a very superficial level. Instead of going into the depths of the longing of the heart, we either privatize it (that is, make it all about ourselves disconnected from the world) or distrust it. This suits the corporate agenda. Let's face it, we are dominated by a set of institutions that want to keep us passive, unfeeling, and dissociated from our own heart and from others, so that the pursuit of the bottom line—at the expense of any real ethical understanding—can go on unchecked. If it continues, the world as we know it will be destroyed.

It isn't just that we've been brainwashed, we have also been programmed. There are powers, be they political, economic, or religious, that not only suppress the wisdom of the heart, but also go so far as to demonize, humiliate, and trash its wisdom. This happens because any relationship in which the heart is not central is then privatized, commercialized, and, as a result, becomes impotent as far as making a difference for justice and solidarity in the world.

When we allow the heart that is within us to be freed, received, honored, and heard, there is a soul-force that is unleashed. This is a soul-force of love that comes out into the world and changes everything. If we suppress the heart, no soul-force is unleashed and nothing happens.

Andrew Harvey: Pierre Teilhard de Chardin said something wonderful: "Some day, after we have mastered the winds, the waves, the tides and gravity, ... we shall harness ... the energies of love. Then, for the second time in the history of the world, man will have discovered fire." This fire is the fire of sacred activism, the third fire that is created from the union of the two noblest fires in the human soul, the fire of the mystic passion for God and the fire of the activist passion for justice. If you are going to awaken the heart, you're going to discover both fires raging in it and you're going to have to do the magnificent work of unifying them.

Also, and this is critical, we have to confront the boiling outrage at the core of our heart, about the rape of the planet, the destruction of the animals, the murder and the genocide and the humiliation of the women and the children. Then we have to do the difficult work of transmuting that outrage into the divine ferocity that feeds from illumined peace but uses a sword to hack through illusion, the sword that Rumi so beautifully describes as a "sword soaked in dawn."

Chris Saade: All over the world, at the grassroots level, we are hearing myriad people say, "Let us go with this idea of the sacred activism of the heart. Let us put love into action in service of peace, democratic freedoms, justice, and inclusion." What is fascinating is that it is coming from people of heart. These are people who are connected with each other through the heart, whether they be Jewish, Christian, Muslim, Hindu, or Bahá'í, etc. They are connected through the heart, irrelevant of their belief system. They are the people who have allowed their own hearts to open up and to feel the incredible pain that is out there, and to feel outrage toward oppression and injustice. For the heart can simultaneously feel peace, joy, grief, passion, and compassion.... This awakening of the heart has propelled them into action, and it has enabled them to connect beyond the divide of all religious dogma. Heart to heart.

Andrew Harvey: Open the heart and you have the most revolutionary force in the world because the force of the heart recognizes no stranger. The force of the heart doesn't ask, "Are you a Muslim or are you a Buddhist or are you a fundamentalist Christian or a non-fundamentalist Christian?" The force of the heart recognizes you as you, as sacred and divine. And the force of the heart says a huge "No" as well as a great "Yes." We've sentimentalized the heart in the New Age outrageously to suit the dumbing down and passivity that is required for us to go stupidly into this terrible, dark night. Through this domesticating and sentimentalizing of the heart we have deprived people of real sacred power— love for one another *and* the transmuted outrage and fierce compassion energy that's born out of real love.

Chris once described to me what happened in Lebanon, how, in the middle of the horror of Beirut, people who were truly awoken to the agony of what was happening, whether they were Muslims or Christians, came together. They came together because they were simultaneously initiated by the heart into a universal compassion and they came together energetically because they were working with their shared outrage at the situation.

Chris Saade: We need people from all over the world to get involved in action, and to feel the heart of God within them as love, outrage, compassion, and passion. Since relationships are one of the essential units of our civilization, we need this passion to serve in order to be at the center of our relationships. If our relationships can get serious about creating a space for each other's heart, we can then link this expanding, unifying movement to the world. Our ability to do this will then enable us to make a hugely positive sociological and ecological difference in the world. And in turn this leads to a relationship that is transfigured by service to the Universe.

Andrew Harvey: To be able to do this, both people have to be mature, brave, and able to deal with intense pain and deep anger. They will have to learn to transmute this pain within themselves and do the work of helping others transmute it also. This requires a level of maturity and a level of commitment that has not yet been in sufficient intensity on the Earth. It is our deepest prayer that this new movement be born now, because it is essential for human survival.

Chris Saade: Amen.

Chapter 6
Advocate Idiosyncratic Differences

The Power of Advocacy
—Andrew Harvey

Chris's passion for advocacy is one of the things that makes me love him. Advocacy is the fourth key. I've been thrilled to hear him speak on this essential key, because very few people are talking about this at the level and with the precision that he brings to it.

My own deep and sometimes painfully lovely experience has taught how essential it is for both people in a sacred evolutionary relationship to be equally committed to supporting each other and encouraging and sustaining each other's efforts in the world.

We need to be committed to remain with each other in celebration, to help each other be steadfast through all the turns of fate. It is essential that both people encourage each other passionately and tenderly through all the challenges of realizing their chosen work. The only way, I believe, for both people to stay in alignment with their sacred mission is to constantly celebrate each other's qualities, efforts, and powers. Otherwise, the whole evolutionary enterprise of relationship will be destroyed.

Practical Tools of Advocacy
—Chris Saade

We are the loving advocates of each other's heart. We are here to bless others—to bless our loved ones, our children, and to bless the world. We need to accept that we can only journey together. That is the meaning of the word *ubuntu* that South African social rights activist Desmond Tutu invokes to us so often; it is together that we can thrive.

It is important to remember that in an evolutionary relationship, the soul of the other needs our support and advocacy, and that our soul needs the support and advocacy from our partner. We do not want to be hijacked into an idea of ourselves as being the one who can do it all on our own—the person with no needs or vulnerabilities. We are very powerful indeed. Yet we are also vulnerable and dependent on the blessings of others; we need our partners.

Advocacy means to fan the flames of each other's heart, and to recognize that task as a spiritual mandate as well as a psychological responsibility. Everyone is responsible for their own passion and their own fire, but we are also here to support each other's enthusiasm and to help each other in this incredible collective struggle that we are going through. In an evolutionary relationship, we hold each other up as we reach to the highest possibility of love-in-action.

To passionately practice advocacy, we need to realize that paradox is part of the structure of the Universe and so is diversity. Diversity within unity—we are all unified in one life and, yet, we are also diverse. Nothing is the same. We have billions of species. We are with people who are diverse. We are with them at work; we are with them in our community; we are with them in the world; we are with them in our relationships. And it is not enough to merely tolerate diversity; we must fall in love with it. We must realize that it is a sacred given that belongs to the Divine itself. The Divine is diverse and united, one and many. This is what we need to know to empower an evolutionary relationship—to be an advocate.

I want to propose some tools here that I think are very powerful. One of them is what I call *unconditional advocacy*. Unconditional advocacy means that when you are with your partner and your partner brings a longing or a position, or says something that you do not resonate with, you remain committed to find one thing in his or her position that you can fully support. You never exile your partner into total otherness. You always say to your partner, "I differ with you on the point you made, however there is something that I'm going to find in your words that I can support, because we are bonded by love and by a common destiny. I'm going to find something in what you are saying that I can learn from and that I can passionately hold up with you."

The second tool is the tool of *honoring,* and it's a very, very ancient tool. Each day, find a quality in your partner that you would be willing to hold up to the light. This is a lesson that we have learned from the American Indians, the ancient Phoenicians and Greeks—the soul needs to be upheld through honoring. Dignity is very important to the soul. There is nothing more romantic, or that touches us more, than when someone we love says to us, "I am so impressed by your courage. I am so touched by your creativity. I so want to honor how you give yourself in service etc..." Attempt to make your honoring as specific as possible—how you work with children, the environment, for social justice, or abuse prevention. Honor your partner's commitment. This is part of an ongoing ritual in an evolutionary relationship.

Another tool is what I call *mirroring greatness.* Take the time to sit with the one you love and feel their greatness in your heart. Go into that deep, deep silence where there is nothing but the experience of the greatness of your beloved. Then say, "I want to mirror back to you that which is so great in your spirit," so that the other can feel their own spirit and its greatness at levels that they have never before felt because they now feel it through you.

The last tool is *romancing the soul.* Romancing the

soul tells the other to what degree they touch and inspire you by what they do. So many times, we do not know how we are touching the other person. We get very little feedback, yet we know that creativity and art is ignited by affirmative feedback. Go to your partner and say, "I want to tell you, when you wrote that chapter and stayed up all night, when you gave of yourself to that older person who needed attention that you lovingly gave your time, this is how it touched me: I felt inspired. My heart expanded. I wrote a piece of music. I wrote a poem." Romance the soul of your partner by sharing the ways in which they inspire you in what they do.

Through advocacy we create bonds. We build bridges. We empower the spirit of the other and it comes back to us tenfold. We keep the romantic fire of the relationship aflame and we invite the spirit of the heart to become the foundation of the relationship and to help hold each of us up. It is tremendously vulnerable and demanding to put ourselves out and to speak heart in our world. It is soul-wrenching to be able to stand up for justice, and to stand for love when there is so much cynicism. We each need the support of our partner to reach to the highest in ourselves. We are *ubuntu*, we need each other; we need each other in words and action. For an evolutionary couple, it is very potent and important to establish these four rituals: unconditional advocacy, honoring, mirroring by greatness, and romancing the soul by telling each other how they touch us. Do these on a weekly basis.

When we do this, we empower ourselves as a couple to serve the world. We also start to realize that it is part of our task to advocate those in the world who are standing for justice and peace. We ask, "This week, who did we support in our community that stands for justice? Who is the teacher in a church, temple, or mosque, who stood up tall and spoke up for peace and justice? Did we advocate them, or did we just leave after they spoke?" This is our responsibility as a couple—the honoring and advocating of others who keep the fire burning.

How to Address the Challenges Related to Advocacy

—A Dialogue between Chris Saade and Andrew Harvey

Andrew Harvey: Let's talk nakedly about the resistances to this advocacy. There are three great sources of resistance. Firstly, we get sabotaged by the nasty voices in ourselves that ask, "Who the hell do you think you are? How dare you stand up and advocate for these things? You're a hypocrite, you're corrupt, you're stupid." That shadow voice also gets projected onto the other. Along with praise for the other, there's the secret inner dialogue which is full of critique.

The second resistance is a result of living in a culture that is entirely structured on competition. Unfortunately, competition infuses nearly all relationships until it's unmasked and unveiled. We can be secretly competitive even in a sacred relationship, and it will deeply corrupt advocacy because we can only wholeheartedly encourage someone else when there is no competition in our mind and heart. We must be solely concentrated on the other and on witnessing their gifts, their inner beauty, and their unique power. If any competitiveness seeps in, it will corrupt the beauty and the power of that advocacy.

The third resistance comes from the addiction to power. We all have in us an ego so devastating that it prefers to humiliate and disempower the other person rather than let them unfold in their full beauty. The sacred evolutionary relationship is not one that pretends that these three kinds of resistance don't exist. It's a relationship that has the courage to really look at these resistances, to suffer through exposing them, and do the grueling work of transmuting them so the full sacred fire of our deepest encouragement of the other can flow lavishly.

Chris Saade: That is so important because if we are not conscious of these voices that sabotage us, our words will not have power or meaning. To say the words without meaning them is horrible, and if we just say nothing, we are indifferent. Holocaust survivor, Elie Wiesel, taught that indifference is the greatest betrayal of the suffering of others. I have to realize that within me, the critical voices never stop. They criticize me; they criticize you; they criticize everything in sight. It's amazing. These voices do not disappear. I've done personal therapy, I have been a therapist, and I have been on this spiritual journey a long time—and these voices are still there. It's like they have their own mechanism.

Andrew Harvey: They are vicious imps that never stop chattering.

Chris Saade: Exactly. But what I can do is make a choice of the heart. I can let these voices say whatever they are going to say, but know that I'm not going to live my life out of that voice. I'm going to live my life out of the voice of the heart, the voice of the spirit, and the deeper voice of the Divine within me. I'm going to offer heartfelt, honoring support to all those around me who are doing their best to love in a very difficult world, who are putting forth their best.

Andrew Harvey: How do we deal with the competition that is so much part of us? What is the alchemy that can transform competitiveness into celebration of each other's heroic virtue?

Chris Saade: For me, I have to admit that I like some competitiveness. I play competitive table tennis. I'm not that good, but I do like the competition. I also have to keep in mind that some competition edges us toward excellence. Competition by constantly pushing our capabilities has its place, but it does not replace the essential fiber of our humanity, which is *ubuntu*, together.

Andrew Harvey: Let's take an example. There is a couple who are dedicated to working with children, and the husband feels that the wife's heart is so much more open than his. He's doing his best and he's really helping, but he sees she has so much more real compassion for the children. He has two possible ways to go. He can feel resentful and begin to hate the thing that he actually loves the most in her—her wise warmth—and that can lead to terrible suffering. Or he can look to his wife as his guru of the heart and say to himself, "How blessed I am to have a woman in my life who shows me who I could be if I opened more." This is where the alchemy of evolutionary love can work. Instead of competing and becoming a saboteur in secret ways, he can use this experience to explore what is blocking him from giving his whole being to it.

Chris Saade: Definitely.

Andrew Harvey: I've seen many men transformed by the women they are in relationship with in this way. Once they take that second route.

Chris Saade: In order to successfully be able to see the other person as our teacher, coach, and friend, there are two things we have to confront. The first is what Andrew speaks about so clearly—we have to be aware of the shadow. We have to be aware that we will always have a voice inside that will resent anyone who does anything better than we do. We simply cannot take it out of ourselves because it is part of our human structure. But we have to decide which voice we allow to rule in our lives. This is when we get to choose the voice that says, "My partner is my beloved, the intimate friend of my heart."

The other issue that is very important is the issue

of need. In psychology, the word *need* has gotten a bad rap. I don't want to be in need of you. I don't want to need you. The myth is that I need to be strong so that I can find everything within myself, as if I was not in an intrinsic relationship with the other and with the world.

Here we must go back to the idea of the paradox: I am strong but I also need you. I need you as my friend on this journey. I need others and their support. I definitely need the support and the love of my partner, and I need to give her love and support in return. When we get overtaken by a sheer competitive attitude, we forget that we need each other in order to live love, serve the world and make a difference.

This has been very important in my life because I love strength. I love to develop my strength, whether it be mental, physical, emotional, or even willpower. I find it fascinating that the Divine has given us great strengths. But at the same time I have to fully acknowledge and respect my unbelievable vulnerability. Without the love and support of others, I am essentially very little, if nothing. I need the other.

Andrew Harvey: At moments of vulnerability we have to make our needs known. We have to go to the loved ones in our life and say, "Please help me in this. Please be with me in this. I love you. I need you. Please, please, stand by me."

Chris Saade: An evolutionary relationship has to create a sacred space for need and not look at it through a negative lens. Strength coexists and dances with need.

Andrew, I love to see you and when I do, I get energy. I need to hear your voice; I need to read your books. I need to be fired up by what you're doing.

Andrew Harvey: And I by you.

Chris Saade: Yes, and that is part of that *ubuntu*, that togetherness. There is a place for competition, to push each other to the best of our abilities, but it needs to be a small place in our lives. The bigger place is for what Andrew calls "networks of grace." Here we stand together and speak out for justice. To speak cynically does not require much. To speak effectively for justice in a way that can transform society requires legions of us—holding together the divine pillar of love for humanity and the Earth.

Andrew Harvey: I think this is the most difficult aspect of our transformation, because until it is understood, most people will be doing their great sacred work alone. This, unfortunately, has been true throughout history. Most of the great prophets and trailblazers have to accept suffering and loneliness as their lot with very little support except from the Divine.

What you and I are really calling for is a revolution in our vision, not only of enlightenment, but also of love relationship. Love can no longer be a place to hide in, but becomes a place in which you make again and again the inner commitment to being the advocate of the other's deepest gifts. It takes fierce courage to keep renewing this commitment to work on anything in yourself that wants in any way to keep the other down or subservient. It is this radical commitment that will, in the end, transform you and your relationship.

Chris Saade: It has been one of the great tragedies of this movement of heart and spirit to see how isolated its pioneers have been. They are either isolated by living alone or, if they are in a relationship, they often remain isolated because there is not a lot of advocacy, honoring, and romancing going on. There is too much silent indifference; it weakens the individual and it limits the potency of the movement for justice, peace, and solidarity. An evolutionary relationship understands how much we need the words of others, the *logos* of others as well as their *eros*. In addition, we need to realize the need we have for their love, attraction, kindness, or friendship.

Andrew Harvey: We need to be seen. We need to be witnessed. We need to have our heroism witnessed. We need to have our agony witnessed. How can we do the great work that we've been called to do to preserve the planet on our own? We have to do it with people who are committed as we are to see the cost and to praise the willingness to pay the price.

Chris Saade: We cannot go nearly as far if we're doing it by ourselves. We have to realize that courage and temerity are extremely important, but a healthy need of others is what weaves us together as a relationship and as a community that can go extremely far.

Andrew Harvey: I'll give you an example from the world of opera. Maria Callas was famously 'challenging' to work with. One day she was asked, "Why have people found you so difficult?" She said, "I want the people singing with me to be as prepared as I am, as dedicated to the score as I am, because I can't carry it alone." Callas knew what revelations of emotional and spiritual truth opera can unleash—but only if all the performers involved assume their responsibilities and marry, as she did, the most exacting discipline to the deepest abandon to the majesty and passion the music is expressing. Callas said to me when I met her months before her death in Paris, "If we are not prepared as musicians both to work on our own flaws of execution incessantly and to surrender to the mystery and power of music itself at ever deeper levels, how can the music of God be played within and through us?"

Chris Saade: Mutual support is what allows us to go beyond the good into greatness. It's what evolutionary couples, and others in relationships, will come to understand together. Then, through our networks with other couples who are also doing this work of the heart, we can move beyond doing ordinary good in the world to doing great in the world.

Chapter 7
Co-Create a Vision of Solidarity

The Power of Co-Creation
—Chris Saade

The fifth key that sustains, nurtures, and empowers an evolutionary relationship is co-creation, in other words, the co-creative attitude.

Before we delve into how we do this, let us look at the context of the idea of co-creation. A couple does not exist in a vacuum or on an island. The privatized idea of relationship will separate the couple from the journey of the world and drain the relationship of its sacred, beautiful, and passionate energy.

An evolutionary couple exists as part of the dream of the Divine for our planet. A couple exists within the greatest epic story ever written; a story I call Project Earth. It is the dream of the Divine for developing upon the Earth a consciousness that can hold love in its full manifestation. This manifestation of love gives birth to freedom, justice, solidarity, peace, inclusion, and compassion—seeking to go to the edges of love's possibilities. Project Earth was conceived some fourteen billion years ago and has been going full steam for the last hundred thousand years.

Today, Project Earth is greatly challenged by the forces that want to reduce this planet to a place of domination and exploitation: "Let's make as much money as we can, as quickly as we can, and not worry about the rest." Our planet is endangered ecologically, politically, economically, and culturally. We, as individuals, as couples, and as families, are part of the great epic journey of reclaiming Project Earth for its initial purpose, which is the development of sacred love in its full manifestation of freedom, justice, peace, and inclusion.

When a couple is co-creating with the Divine and with others of a similar heart and spirit who love freedom and justice, they are co-creating with the Divine in a vision of healing and transformation on a societal level. The couple needs to understand its place in this great big unfolding. They are, as a unit, co-creating visions that uphold love-in-action, that uphold freedom and justice in the world.

For this to be achieved, the couple has to start by consciously adopting a co-creative attitude, which is an attitude that rejects the sense that it has to be "my way." Co-creation recognizes that if one person gets "their way," they have lost, because it is the fusion of various energies that makes for the ultimate good, the ultimate best for the relationship and for our planet. We have to speak our authenticity yet be eager to have a co-creation happen that merges the essence of many authenticities into a higher and more potent synthesis.

The co-creative person and the co-creative couple

are consciously seeking to invite and meld together the desires of their partner with those of their own. From both desires, they seek to unfold a co-creative breakthrough that can hold the essence of both, but that can also go beyond it. This allows them, within the relationship itself, to create a space that is fully respectful of the truth of each, and also fully open to the breakthrough of divine love and divine intelligence through co-creation. This is strength, openness, and flexibility joined together.

Now let us take this a bit further. From this co-creative attitude, the couple can then ask, "How can we, as a couple, co-create a vision of service for the world? What do we desire to do in the world?" Some of it they will do by themselves, independently. However, some of it can be done as a co-created vision of the couple.

To do this, a couple needs to keep on remembering they are part and parcel of the service of the world. Relationships carry within themselves not only the joys of the world, but the hopes, aspirations, and pain of the world. The world lives within us. The suffering of the world exists within us and within our relationship. Out of that brokenness we can find intelligence, energy, and the vision to develop the will to make a difference in the world. To do this is to heal and enrich ourselves as we are contributing to the world, because we and the world are never separate.

I want to share with you an exercise that can be very powerful within a relationship. The couple comes together at a time when they have the ability to create a peaceful moment in their lives. They sit together in silence and look into each other's eyes. Each of them connects intimately with the heart of the Divine and allows themselves to have a passionate connection; a fusion of intimacy with the heart of the Divine.

After really breathing in and feeling the lover-to-lover connection with the divine Heart, the couple repeats the same exercise, but this time each enters into a passionate, intimate relationship with the soul of the world. Each feels oneness with the struggles of the world, as well as the hopes, aspirations, pain, brokenness, and the tenacity of the world. Each feels the oneness that they have as individuals with the soul of the world. They experience how they are one with every attempt from the past, present, and future to bring justice and compassion into the world. Each becomes one with the tears, prayers, and brokenness—to the breakthroughs of the world. After experiencing this intimate connection with the heart and soul of the world, they again look at each other in silence, holding hands and allowing this fusion and passionate connection to enter the heart of their connection together. Afterward they share their experience with each other and underline common issues that are calling on them both.

This exercise helps a couple create the space, energy, and co-creative vision to serve the world while realizing that their source—undying, unchangeable, and unstoppable love—is the Divine. They can pull all the power of the love from that source and pour it into the relationship.

Let us always remember that we are called to become co-creators of justice and peace as individuals, couples, families, and communities—wherever we are in relationship. We are called to join hands and hearts, and together create and implement a vision of service in the world.

Co-Creation in Partnership with the Divine
—Andrew Harvey

A co-creative couple commits to being unified with the soul of the world and its epic evolutionary struggle to be embodied and realized in every institution, in every dimension, in every way of being and doing, all over the world. This dream is enshrined in all of the great visions of evolution of all of the great mystical traditions: in Jesus's vision of the Kingdom, in the Kabbalistic vision of the Messiah, in the Tibetan Buddhist vision of Shambhala. At the core of our evolutionary journey is this desire of God to create with us and through us the Kingdom/Queendom on Earth, a totally integrated vision of compassion and justice in action, that springs from loving, committed, human beings coming together in love, to do the real sacred work of establishing the divine laws of justice and compassion in every realm of Earth life.

So what does it mean to ground the relationship in

the Divine? You can only have a co-creative relationship with another human being at the level that we're talking about and praying for, if the Divine is made a conscious partner in that relationship by both people. And the way I envisage it is as a pyramid. The two people are the base of the pyramid and the Divine at the top of the pyramid is the constant reference of both people, individually and together. Without that constant, subtle invocation of the Divine to penetrate and suffuse and inspire every single aspect of the relationship, an evolutionary relationship is not possible. You will not be able to sustain the rigors, stresses, ecstasies, revelations, passions, transformations, of a real evolutionary love unless both people have a material spiritual practice, separately and together, and unless both people have, in the deepest part of themselves, dedicated their love for the other to the realization of the Divine in themselves, in the other, and in the world.

One of the great blocks to an authentic co-creative attitude is the rampant narcissism of what is called the inner child relationship with God. Fundamentally, the narcissism of the self-proclaimed divine child works itself out in the following way: We are of the Divine. God will look after us. It's all in divine order. We don't have to transform ourselves. We don't have to change. We don't have to go through the death/rebirth crucifixion/resurrection process of the mystical path. All we have to do is to basically turn up as relatively decent people with a few mantras and God will do the rest because God's job is to be a perfectly indulgent, benign, infinite, benevolent, father/mother. And our job is just to sit there and receive these astounding gifts.

This is tragic and absurd because it is passive and un-transforming, an abomination which portrays God as a kind of sanctified servant, ready to do whatever you want, and manifest whatever you desire. This is a blasphemy against the Divine/human relationship. It's a total misrepresentation of the authentic co-creative attitude, which depends upon our whole being's embrace of the freedom that the Divine has given us and the ongoing responsibility to use that freedom justly.

This freedom has two potential forks in the road. One leads to dark freedom that creates out of the unexamined drive to power of the unhealed ego. It's quite clear what that freedom has led to—a suicidal, matricidal situation, in which we are killing ourselves and killing the environment. This is the disaster of our evolutionary refusal to take responsibility for this freedom.

The other path leads to a sometimes frightening and adult acceptance of divine freedom as the supreme grace. What it allows us to do, if we really do the work of aligning with the Heart of hearts and with the soul of the world, is to become conscious, dazzled, divine children, in the highest sense, playing in the fields of life with divine inspiration, with divine love, with divine energy, with divine peace.

But the problem with this freedom, and the problem that has preoccupied people about this freedom, is that it requires profound responsibility. Once you have glimpsed the fact that God has given you the potential to be, as the Sufis say, the vice-regent of the world, the guardian of the world, you have to step up. You have to take on the burden and the pain and the difficulty, as well as the rapture, of that responsibility. You have to realize that every thought you think, every action you do, every time you let your shadow dominate without being scrupulous about it, you are creating karmic consequences. To be a co-creator without incurring devastating karmic consequences to yourself, both individually and as a couple, you must constantly work on claiming your authentic responsibility to the world and really doing your inner work to make sure your will, both individually and as a couple, is as clearly focused on the Divine will as possible.

There is no co-creation without total surrender to the Divine. This is one of the great paradoxes the New Age has been totally inept at uncovering. Those who are co-creators with the Divine of a new reality, are not working from their egos. They have surrendered to the Beloved. They have gone through the burning process of the authentic mystical path. Their full selves have been dissolved, so that who they truly are takes over. Only at this high stage is co-creation possible, because at that stage what is being co-created with God is God's own will for your life, for your destiny, for your mutually shared path.

The New Age has told people, "Oh, we're co-creators right now just as we are." But we only become authentically co-creative when we have truly surrendered our ego to the self, our ego to the soul. Everything done before that stage has inevitable darkness and shadows. We cannot co-create with the Divine unless we co-create with the complete Divine. If we only co-create with what we imagine to be the light, the love, the spaciousness, the peace, the rapture of the Divine, it can take us quite far. But if we want to co-create with God a new world, both individually and as a couple, we have to find the strength to open to the heartbreak of God— heartbreak at injustice, at cruelty, at the madness of this fundamentalism of the bottom line that dominates our commercial culture. It's this heartbreak that will drive us to give more and more, separately and together, to the world. This heartbreak is not something to be afraid of, it's not something to deny; it is, as all of the greatest mystics of love have told us, something we can learn to bless and embrace as the source of our most potent creativity in the world.

If we're not heartbroken at the state of the poor, we'll never galvanize our energies to do anything about it. If we're not heartbroken at what's happening to the animals, we'll never find the courage to stand up and witness the truth of the holiness of animals and call for a revolution in our relationship with them. If we're not heartbroken at the way in which women have been raped, degraded, and humiliated, we will never find it in ourselves, either as a woman or as a man, to really integrate the sacred truths of the Divine Feminine and stand up for the social and political changes that are essential to honor them. If we're not heartbroken at the way in which gay people have been degraded and downtrodden, we will never be able to really stand in solidarity with our gay brothers and sisters and celebrate their brave creativity. The New Age refusal to look at so-called negative emotions or the darkness in reality in the name of an adoration of the light side of God, is actually an insurance that the true birth will not take place. Without the passion energy that comes from heartbreak, the energy that streams from the light cannot co-create a new world.

Co-Creation in the Context of Our Evolution
—A Dialogue between Andrew Harvey and Chris Saade

Chris Saade: It is fascinating how we are evolving into knowing ourselves as co-creators with the fullness of the love emerging from the Divine. We have historically developed the ability to create independently, which is a God-given force within us; but now we are evolving, becoming co-creators, and realizing that we need each other to achieve the highest manifestation of love, freedom, and justice in the world. This is opening an incredible chapter for us in the history of relationships because what two people generate is more than the sum of their energies. It is exponential. When we go into co-creation, we release exponential energy.

Andrew Harvey: It's like chemistry. When you bring two potent substances together, the result is a quantum leap in power.

Chris Saade: Yes, very much so. I'm thinking about when Jesus said, "For where two or three are gathered together in my name, there am I in the midst of them" (King James Version, Matt. 18:20). I believe he is saying that in the name of this fullness of love, we are empowered. He also says, "Lo, I am with you always, even unto the end of the world" (Matt. 28:20). Meaning, we have divine support to do all that we need to do in life even through the greatest challenges. We are in a great partnership of love. But it will only happen when we get out of that privatized sense of isolation and enter into full co-creation with divine love and with others. Our unique sense of authenticity is undoubtedly crucial, but it can flower only through the generosity of love. As unique authentic individuals we enter into a deeper relationship with ourselves through our passion for Project Earth.

Andrew Harvey: Because we're going to be talking about sexuality in the next dialogue, it is important to understand that, at the deepest level, the real destination of authentic tantric sexuality—the abandonment of one being to another in ecstasy—isn't the savoring of that ecstasy in the relationship alone. It is that the tremendous erotic energy inspires both people to become erotic towards the world, erotic towards justice, erotic towards animals, and towards compassion in its fullest.

It is training in the divine Eros that opens you to the expanded reaches of that Eros. Justice is Eros in action. Compassion is Eros in action. The whole point of rousing divine sexuality is to give people the fuel to create and sustain this force of sacred activism so they have the energy and inspiration to co-create together.

Chris Saade: We are beginning to see more and more that everything is interconnected and interdependent. We are breaking out of the eighteenth-century false myth of the privatized and separate way of being. For example: regarding our sexuality we need to remember that the powerful and beautiful energy that we access through a healthy sexuality is for our own enjoyment as individuals and as a couple but is also an energy that needs to translate itself as an offering to the world of creativity and service. Any energy we access is at the same time ours and also belongs to the world. Any blessings we have are for us and also are meant to gift the world. The couple is part of the entire web of connection.

Taking this relationship out of the great web of connection and putting it on an island and scrutinizing it as if it existed by itself, is a violation of the essence of evolutionary love.

Andrew Harvey: The whole point of an evolutionary relationship is to give both people a joyful experience of stability and peace, and also to energize, stabilize, empower, and inspire both people to create the great interconnected unit of a grand evolutionary adventure.

Chris Saade: Saint Francis of Assisi, and so many other heart-centered spiritual teachers, believed and still believe in the tremendous gifts we are given when we act for others. I believe that by passionately giving from our true authenticity, we grow in strength. When a couple allows themselves to be connected to the hope and aspirations contained within the heart and soul of the Divine, in addition to the brokenness within our world, what they receive back is tenfold to a hundredfold in energy. It provides a necessary sense of meaning, a galvanizing and creative stimulation, which allows the couple to fall in love with each other again and again. We cannot stress enough that this source is love—divine love—present everywhere and within everything.

Andrew Harvey: The ultimate word for God in the Koran is "generous." When a couple evolves this conscious co-creation with God, they experience not only the rapture of giving but also the rapture in the heart of God. God's gifts become consciously known and then consciously returned in service and love. This is a huge potential opening for the human being.

Chris Saade: It is very transformative. Couples benefit greatly from sitting together and reflecting together upon all these aspects of enchanting and powerful love—authenticity, paradox, the heart, advocacy, co-creation, and later we will be talking about celebration. These principles are life giving. They won't suddenly solve every problem and create a panacea because we are still part of the struggle of humanity. Any relationship, however excellent it is, will still carry challenges and moments of difficulty. Excellence is not perfection. It is an arc imperfectly bending toward a beautiful evolutionary vision. It is growth through the paradoxes of our humanity. Our hearts need to be wide enough to carry—with respect—the ups and downs of the progression of the waves of partnership. We can be at peace within ourselves, but we still have to struggle with our shadows, with voices of oppression interjected into our minds, and brokenness. These principles open up a limitless source of passion and blessing. The practice of these principles enables us to move from a suffocating and privatized isolated relationship into an evolutionary relationship. As we do this we grow toward one of the highest forms of existence on Earth—a life of authenticity wedded with solidarity: love as the union between the freedom of individual authenticity with the passion for global solidarity.

Chapter 8
Celebrate

Celebration
—Andrew Harvey

In a time as dangerous, dissociated, depressing, and depressed as ours, where people are in a terrible funk of paralysis and despair at the exploding world crisis, it is essential to make a radical commitment to celebration. Anyone who wants to live a life of evolutionary love with another person must be radically committed to celebration, because this is the only way to connect the couple to the essential nature of the Father/Mother, the essential nature the Hindus call *ananda*, "the great bliss." All the mystics of all the traditions have said with one voice that when you truly connect with the heart of the Divine in its ultimate essence, what you experience is ecstasy and bliss. They also say with one voice that the way to keep that connection vibrant is through gratitude, gratitude for everything—for the whole gift of being alive, for the gift of being a human being with divine consciousness, for the gift of the grasses and the flowers, and the skies and the seas, and the dolphins and the whales and the orchids, for everything including the chaos, horror, and ferocious suffering that are also part of the Holy Alchemy of the One.

In the Shvetashvatara Upanishad, which is one of my favorite of all religious texts, this truth of the essential nature of God and its power to invigorate even in the most disastrous circumstances is given so beautifully: "The Universal Soul exists in every individual, it expresses itself in every creature. Everything in the world is a projection of it and there is Oneness, a unity of souls in one and only Self." Discover and live the self – I know this now through the grace of the divine – and you will experience a stable grounded peace and a strong and serene joy whatever is happening in the world.

There's a Hindu story of an old Brahmin, Bhrigu Varuni, who says to his son, whom he loves, and whom he wishes to see awaken before he dies, "Go off and meditate and come back and tell me what you discover." His son comes down from the mountain and says, "Oh Dad, I've got the secret of life. The essence of life is food." Well, that's not quite the answer, so Dad says, "Go back, go back, meditate further, plunge deeper." This goes on for six or seven wonderful answers, which are close to the truth, but not the truth.

Then one day Bhrigu Varuni sees his son come down the mountain and he sees that he's radiant and peaceful, and the old man's heart is filled with rapture because he knows his son now knows. He goes up to his son and says, "I know you know, but before I die I just want to hear from your lips what you have discovered." And his son says, "From the great bliss, all things have come; in the great bliss, all things are sustained; and to the great bliss all things return. This is the highest mystical teaching."

If you can make this radical commitment to celebration, you will find that the gift of that commitment will be, for you, a direct connection to that all-embracing, all-transforming, all-invigorating joy that is behind all the dance of the world. A wonderful image of this is the image of *Shiva Nataraja*. In one hand, Shiva has the flame of destruction, and in the other hand he has the drum of creation, but if you look carefully at the statue, you'll see that his face radiates a royal serene bliss that embraces both creation and destruction, while transcending them. To live from the always flowing energy of this royal bliss is the work of evolutionary love, a work that enables us both to embrace and transcend duality as the divine dancer does. Such a demanding work needs to be fed and sustained by a steady passion of celebration.

There are five kinds of celebration a couple needs to practice effortlessly and seamlessly, with great humor and with great intelligence in the course of their love journey. First, they must celebrate together the gorgeous power and beauty of the Divine. If you want a beloved-beloved relationship with another human being, root it in a constant celebration of a Beloved-beloved relationship with God. Then the great wisdom and peace of that relationship will flood your relationship.

The second celebration that is crucial is to celebrate the wonder of being with another human being who is willing, despite your faults and your craziness and your comic complications, to say to you, "Not only do I love you, but I want to go on a journey to divinization with you to become a being who can radiate the fierce and tender love of God in works of justice and compassion for the world." This will always remind you of what an extraordinary grace it is to meet someone with whom you can attempt to live this sacred relationship. Celebrating the fact that he or she has turned up in your life will give you the courage to go through all the stresses of actually sorting out the difficulties of the relationship. What greater grace could you be given than meeting a potent beloved partner in the journey to divinization? Celebrate that grace and it will grow.

The third kind of celebration is a celebration of all those things in ordinary life that can so easily become banal. One of the great things that happened to me by living in Paris was that I understood how so-called "ordinary" pleasures can be experienced from the awakened heart as subtle divine revelations. A simple lunch for your beloved can become a form of ecstatic prayer. A walk in the park can become holy communion. Make every occasion you share with the one you love an occasion to celebrate simply the magnificence, the benevolence of the Universe that presents you with the joy of being together.

The fourth kind of celebration involves embracing the chaos, the horror, the difficulty, the agony, the heartbreak of the Divine as well as the ecstasy and joy and bliss of the Divine. One of the things that the couple really needs to celebrate are the defeats, the failures, the difficulties that arise, and the shadows of each other.

You can find your way to celebrate a failure in communication, for example, if it led to both people examining their motives and their shadows more deeply. And if it led to more vulnerability between both people, then that led to a deeper compassion. In celebrating this you are celebrating the fundamental alchemical rhythm of evolution, and it will become more and more obvious to you that God is appearing in your relationship, not just as the highs, but also as the lows, not just as the joys, but also as the griefs, and that those griefs are not blocks, not obstacles, but fierce opportunities for deeper truth and deeper realization.

The fifth kind of celebration is to really celebrate when the power and beauty and evolutionary intensity of the relationship enable you to create something amazing in the world together, to really celebrate the divine blessing of being in a couple that can co-create in this way.

I have very close friends who are like brother and sister to me, and they've been patrons of sacred activism. She made a great deal of money in stocks, and he was the head of a corporation who got wise about what corporations are up to and left because he wanted a richer and deeper life. The two of them have joined forces to be potent philanthropists on a global scale.

Whenever something wonderful happens as a result of their generosity, they have a party and they celebrate, not the fact that they're wealthy, and not the fact that they've had the good intentions to do something, but the power of love to really change things. The people who have been helped are invited, and what's made clear to them is that by being able to help, my friends have been profoundly helped and transformed in their own right. From their wisdom, from their humility, I have learned just how powerful this kind of celebration can be.

Unify these five kinds of celebration in your life and whatever happens to you through sickness and defeat and grief and loneliness and mutual alienation at times, you will find that you will be connecting your whole reality with the Father/Mother through the golden thread of Divine Love and its all-transforming *ananda*.

The Crucial Importance of Celebration
—Chris Saade

Three words: Celebrate, celebrate, celebrate! To undertake this epic journey and to become fully involved in the struggle of creating love in the world, we have to be able to dance our celebrations in the midst of the greatest of challenges and struggles. Without celebration, we will not be able to advance.

Emperor Julian was a third-century Roman Emperor. He was a fascinating historical figure—visionary, tolerant, very present in his body, lover of the Earth. During his reign he reverted to paganism rather than continuing to follow Christianity in the footprints of his predecessors. His rationale for shying away was due to the lacks he saw within Christians during his day. They didn't celebrate the body, the mind, and the heart. They saw the "self "as being defective and unworthy. For us this is not necessarily about Paganism versus Christianity. It is a reminder of the importance of participating in the great epic journey of love with the realization that we, as individual human beings, in our bodies, minds, and hearts are worthy of celebration and are a very important part of divine love. In our authentic selves, we are grounded in an unborn and undying love. We are part of an indestructible story. Our great worth and sense of dignity are not determined by results. Results are very circumstantial. There are times to sow, times to reap, and there are times where we are not able to sow the ground or reap the fruits. However, whatever happens, our sense of worth and dignity is fed by who we are in the authenticity of our unique selves. We are each a unique manifestation of divine presence and divine love. We have been crafted through hundreds of millions of years of evolution. Our psyche, our body, our mind, our hearts, and our personality have been fashioned by this long stretch of evolution. The Universe has invested a great deal in us. So when we live from the heart, when we live in harmony with our true authenticity of self, when we dedicate our freedom to the nobility of global justice and global solidarity, regardless of what happens, we partake in the glory of the human journey and thus of the spiritual journey.

We are simply reminded of the importance of entering this epic journey with the realization that we are part of a dream of the Divine that cannot be thwarted. The consciousness of peace and justice will develop, even though precisely when, where, and how is beyond our present understanding. But we can face the problems with the realization of who we are in the depth of our spirit. We are a majestic presence and a miraculous manifestation of the love of the Divine. This realization offers a great moment to say, "Stop everything. Let's celebrate."

It's very important for a couple to find as many occasions as possible to celebrate their relationship as it engages in the great dream of love—love for each other and love for the world. Celebration cannot only be sentimental and incidental. Often, it is helpful to treat it as a ritual, designed and intentionally called forth. It must be planned—once a week, twice a week, the first Monday of each month. It of course can be spontaneous but with our busy schedules, and our orientation toward depreciating the self, we may find it necesary to set regular times to celebrate, celebrate, celebrate!

Celebration must not be isolated and privatized. Birthdays, Thanksgiving, and other sacred times of celebration can also be times to affirm the collective journey toward justice and peace. If you are throwing a birthday party for your beloved or for your child, take a moment to acknowledge the nobility of your partner, of your son or your daughter. Celebrate their contributions to building the world that the Divine Love dreams of, and celebrate the individual as part of that great unfolding story.

I recommend celebrations every other week of the relationship itself. Share them together or invite others. Surprise your friends with an invitation to a special celebration—with or without a specific reason. Our beings deserve plenty of honoring and recognition. Celebrate other couples who are engaged in the world.

Also, celebrate the breakthroughs happening in your

community. When we celebrate something, we make it stronger. We infuse it with life. We root it in the heart of the Divine by rooting it within our own, and we make it flower. I was a consultant in Charlotte, North Carolina, in an amazing grief center called "The Respite." It is a place that held the sacredness of grief and honored how grief serves as a wellspring of great creativity and service. Find things in your community that are happening in service of others and of the world. Bring people to the light who are making things happen—within your relationships, family, community, et cetera—love grows when it is intentionally and openly celebrated. Children especially grow strong and wise as their spirits and gifts are celebrated, loudly and proudly.

Celebration is a form of blessing. When I say I want to celebrate you, it means I want to bless the self that you are, the self that is emanating love, and the self that is working for the world. Blessing emanates from a source of power that is beyond the reach of commercialism. It is based on the power of the soul and is one of the greatest powers the soul possesses. You have that power. Celebration is like watering a flower. You have the power to celebrate and help that flower grow.

Also, the celebration of defeats is crucial. By celebrating defeat, we tell ourselves and the world that defeat is sacred. No great project can be undertaken without many defeats. Abraham Lincoln experienced unbelievable defeats. At first, he couldn't even get elected into Congress. Gandhi also experienced incredible defeats in his life, some of which were related to his immediate family. Mother Teresa struggled with depression. Every great seeker, creator, and pioneer will encounter many defeats on their journey forward. Nietzsche, whose books posthumously sold in the millions, first had to print his own copies and beg his friends to read them because he couldn't sell them. Any great creation in the world for peace, justice, and solidarity will involve great defeats.

A couple who is desiring an evolutionary relationship will experience many setbacks on their way forward. But these defeats are part of the regeneration of this creative process. They are like a necessary dark color in a painting, without it there is no depth. Defeats are not an unfortunate detour. They are part and parcel of creation and co-creation. That is why they are so important.

I have a very good friend, a leader in the work of bringing together spirituality, psychology, and social activism. She raised her children with these principles. Her daughter had an important breakdown in her life. My friend went to her daughter and said, "Tonight I'm inviting you to a great celebration." Her daughter, who was in a bad place at that moment, was perplexed. "What is there to celebrate?" she asked. Her mother said, "We going to have an amazing dinner, on me, to celebrate your defeat. Your defeat is a part of your passion for life—a passion I greatly respect." She did this because within defeat resides real heroism. Defeats are part of the creative momentum. So, get together once or twice a month, name your defeats, and celebrate them.

Another time to celebrate is when you undertake a project, sometime before you finish it. By celebrating before the aimed for result is attained, you celebrate the process of creative manifestation. Let's say you are writing a book or creating an after-school program for children in your community, and you are not sure of the results. By celebrating before you know how things will turn out, you are declaring that this project is part of an emanation of love, no matter the results. It is very important to have a celebration that does not depend upon results. Otherwise you are saying that only results are worthy of celebration, rather than honoring the courageous and often heroic efforts of the soul.

It is important not only to celebrate if your child gets an "A." It is important that you celebrate the efforts your child makes to go for the best in themselves and to make a difference in the world. Ideally, celebration happens many times before the result is evident. In this way, we are not dependent upon results. It is the sacred process that is celebrated.

Celebration springs from a deep sense of gratitude and worship. It is a realization that at the core of ourselves is the joy of being loved by the Divine because we are partners with the Divine. We are part of the divine dream of love that no one and nothing can take away. Our worth springs from the truth of our being and the affirmation of our authenticity.

Throughout my experiences during the war in Lebanon, while I was working in peace organizations, I saw my city destroyed. I saw incredible suffering. Yet within and around that suffering, there was a presence of the Divine that no one could ever take away. I learned during these tragic years that there is a beautiful strength within us if we stay true to our authenticity—a strength that connects us with the luminosity of life—whatever the circumstances. A strength that incorporates our resilience as well as our vulnerability, our successes as well as our set backs. That strength of spirit needs to be unconditionally celebrated in ourselves, our partners, our children, and our friends. So, remember the importance of celebration and how it can empower you and those around you. Celebrate individually and as a couple. Set times for celebration. Get it onto your calendar. Celebrate, celebrate, celebrate!

My wish for you is that celebration remains the morning dew that continuously waters and nurtures your relationship.

The Playfulness and Sacred Joy of Celebration
—A Dialogue between Chris Saade and Andrew Harvey

Andrew Harvey: One of my closest friends on Earth rang me up the other day and said, "I've been reading your books, and I love your books. I love the kind of evolutionary vision you have. But there's one word you never use. It's so unusual that you don't use it, because, when you are on form, you're a living example of it." She added, "That word is *fun*!"

Part of celebration is fun and playfulness. One of the most enchanting aspects of His Holiness the Dalai Lama's character, is his endless, irrepressible, divine sense of fun. It bubbles up constantly from him and is one of the deepest reasons he is so loved and trusted. Holiness and hilarity dance together in him to invite us into the freedom he radiates.

What cripples so many couples is a dreary, high seriousness about everything. I don't want people to read this book and think, "My god, the evolutionary adventure just involves all of this strenuous practice, strenuous facing of the shadow." The only way you can ever leaven the necessary rigor of a real evolutionary journey is by making sure that your appetite for fun is released. This is an essential part of the Divine Child—the child plays, the child sings, the child rejoices, the child dances. I love the French word, *jouissance*; it means savoring with delight. See that your lives together are filled with as many occasions for *jouissance* as you can find and create. The struggles you'll have to go through will be sweetened and leavened.

Chris Saade: Definitely. We are called to love life and love our destiny. We are on Earth to co-create with the Divine. This great dream involves a great struggle. This is what life is, why not love this life and find the pleasures and joys within, rather than perceive the journey as a dreary story? In this struggle we are called to love life, celebrate—laughing whenever we can—because this is our life.

We are here to build something beautiful and momentous in the world. Great! Let's do it, but let's do it with tremendous abandon, surrender, enjoyment, fun, pleasure, and laughter.

Andrew Harvey: It won't be divine if we don't. One of the things I discovered, especially when I was writing *The Hope*, actually it was a revelation to me, came while I was working on the last chapter, "The Law of Joy." I got all my laws together and I really meditated.

"There is something wrong with this," I thought. "There is something missing." Then I had a dream, and in the dream I saw Shiva the Dancer turn into the Divine Child. I realized that what was missing from the vision of sacred activism that I was presenting was the joy of the Divine Child, a bubbling playful joy without which the grueling work of constantly turning up to serve humanity can make us resentful, exhausted, and burned-out. We're called to be both divine dancer and divine child. What characterizes divine creativity is a smile, is play, is a mysterious lightness grounded in and flowing from the solid serenity of divine wisdom.

Chris Saade: I have found in my practice that two things stop people from being able to celebrate and cause them to become overly serious about the journey. First, they become overly serious about the difficulties and the defeats. A lot of people find it extremely hard to accept the defeats that are part and parcel of the creative journey.

Andrew Harvey: The evolutionary journey above all. My God, we're constantly failing. If we're not failing often, we can't evolve since it is very often our failures that initiate our deepest realizations and spur us forward into richer surrender and more conscious inner and outer work.

Chris Saade: If we realize that defeats and losses are part of the sacred journey, then defeats are sacred and dignified and can be celebrated. If not, defeats will be a nemesis on the journey.

Andrew Harvey: Right. If you take defeat too seriously, if you take it too personally, if you don't realize that in the evolutionary journey defeat is inevitable, failure is inevitable.

Chris Saade: It is inevitable, but it is also gorgeous. When we are watching a movie, for example, about Albert Einstein, Thomas Edison, or Marie Curie and we see them going through so many defeats, we actually enjoy the movie more. We see it fully..."What a beautiful movie it is that includes these defeats."

We need to look at our own life this way, and realize that these defeats are truly gorgeous when viewed from the eyes of the eternal, the dream, the Divine.

So, the second thing that blocks people from being able to celebrate is facing the difficulties. Difficulties become so overwhelming for us because we do not realize that facing difficulties is like the training of an Olympian. Olympic athletes learn to love the difficulties and to love the challenge. We have to find in ourselves the love of the challenge.

Andrew Harvey: The Eros of the challenge.

Chris Saade: Yes. The Eros of the challenge.

Andrew Harvey: The difficulties become like clumsy moments in lovemaking; they become spurs to a greater intensity.

Chris Saade: So true. Once we can accept, and moreover

honor, these defeats and difficulties and see them as part of the great Eros, a part of the great sacred beautiful and meaningful dance of life, then we can start enjoying life. Nietzsche taught us the importance of loving life as it is. We need to learn to love our life with its blessings and lacks, successes and gut wrenching defeats. They are all part of our sacred story. Like a mother and father who are dedicated to their children, they love everything about that baby, everything. They adore that baby. There is nothing they don't love about that baby.

Andrew Harvey: I feel that way about my cats.

Chris Saade: Yes, that's how you feel about your cats, exactly, and so do people feel who love their dogs. Once we love and allow the passion of love to flow, there is nothing in our partner, or in life, that is not lovable (of course, with the exception of abuse). When a difficulty or a defeat overwhelms us, it means we have not fully accessed this heroic love that the Divine has been filling us with for fourteen billion years.

Love transforms everything. It does not stop defeat or the dog from peeing on your favorite carpet. However, when the dog that you adore pees on your favorite carpet, it's a whole different story. You're frustrated, but you're also smiling affectionately, whether overtly or covertly.

Andrew Harvey: Rilke has this wonderful line in one of his last poems, *The Sonnets to Orpheus*. He says, "Nur im Raum der Rühmung darf die Klage gehen."

It is only in the room of praise that lamentation should go. So even lamentation, that deep, visceral distress, is actually an embryonic form of praise. It's the beginning of the longing for completion and wholeness that can take you to a new level of evolution.

Chris Saade: In the tradition of great warriors, when they are going into a battle they know they cannot win, they still choose to fight to protect their community, even knowing they will die. The evening before, not only do they pray, but they bathe and make themselves beautiful. They adorn themselves with gorgeous clothing—to gallantly face their destiny.

There is a Phoenician fairy tale I remember being told by elders when I was growing up. I will recount it to you to the best of my memory. In it, a warrior sends his child home, because he knows there is impending death awaiting him and his fellow soldiers who are guarding the gate. He tells his son that he will be forever in his heart… that love is unending, then he sends the child home to his mother. Hesitating to leave, the child asks why the father is anointing himself and making himself look his best if he is going to die. The father replies that it is because the oil smells wonderful and that one lives and dies in the pride of who one is. His father shares that he is only willing and able to face his own death while celebrating the ultimate beauty of his body and soul. Unwilling to meet his demise with anything less than complete dignity and honor, he asks his son to remember this lesson—face life and death with pride and beauty, so that anyone witnessing it will not be able to deny the splendor of your heart.

Andrew Harvey: I remember being at the funeral of a man in his nineties who'd been a great writer and artist, and who'd had the most extraordinary relationship with his surviving widow. At the funeral, his widow broke down and sobbed and sobbed and sobbed. It was the most devastating sound that I'd ever heard, but it was also the most beautiful.

Chris Saade: Oh, yes.

Andrew Harvey: I was with her, and I was accompanying her, and I didn't try and console. Later she told me, "I am so grateful that I could cry like that, because my grief isn't just for losing him. It is a celebration of everything that we shared." When you can find that conjunction of opposites, that ecstasy of pain and that joy in grief, then you are beginning to be really free.

Chris Saade: That is so important, Andrew. When grief is seen as sacred and beautiful, only then can we understand how life is fundamentally gorgeous. That is the huge next evolutionary step for us. When she said, "My grief is a celebration of the person," we understand that in the great mystery of life, tears are also jewels.

Andrew Harvey: As you speak, Chris, these ravishing words of Rumi ring in my heart:

> *I am in love with my pain and my suffering*
> *So I can delight my matchless King*
> *I turn grief's dust into collyrium for my eyes*

So their two seas can fill with pearls
Tears that his creatures weep for him are pearls—
Never say with fools that they are only tears.

Section 3

Eros and Evolutionary Sexuality

Chapter 9
Delving into the Fullness of Sacred Sexuality

The Concept of Evolutionary Sexuality
—Andrew Harvey

L et me begin by sharing two texts that have been thrilling guides for me into the revelation of Tantra. They are from the Vijnana Bhairava Tantra, perhaps the greatest of all Hindu explorations of the world of blissful energy tantra can initiate us into. The translations are by Lorin Roche in his great book, *The Radiance Sutras,* that should be in the backpack of the sacred heart of every evolutionary adventurer.

> *As the fires build in sexual joy*
> *Enter that blessed place between the legs*
> *Embrace the holy energy shimmering there.*
>
> *Follow the rising flow,*
> *undulating throughout the spine,*
> *Shivering with pleasure.*

As the fire intensifies
And flashes upwards
Suspend the breath for a moment.
Throw your whole self in.

Become brilliance in your bodily form,
In union with primordial bliss.

* * * * * * * * * * * * * * * * * * * *

At the moment of orgasm
The truth is illumined—
The one everyone longs for.

Lovemaking is riding the currents of excitation
Into revelation.
Two rivers run together,
The body becomes quivering.

No inside and no inside—
Only the delight of union.
The mind releases itself into divine energy,
And the body knows where it comes from.

This is reality, and it is always here.
Everyone craves the Source
And it is always everywhere.

Evolutionary sexuality takes *Tantra* to the next level. It celebrates what Tantra celebrates, which is making love as an act of ecstatic worship that unifies with the

Father/Mothers' bliss energies, but it doesn't privatize that initiation. In evolutionary sexuality two beings worship each other as divine archetypes and dedicate that worship to the birth of justice and compassion in a restored and renovated world. This is what makes it evolutionary in the fullest sense.

Tantric sexuality on its own can build a vibrant, solid, glorious sense of the Divine living in you and in the other, but it can be limited and dangerous if that's where it ends. The whole point of feeling that power, that glory, that peace, that radiance in every cell of your being is to make you a lover warrior for the future of the planet.

As this conversation between Chris and me unfolds, we'll be exploring sexuality as abandoned and tender worship, but we'll be constantly stressing in different ways how this glorious empowerment that comes from the *Tantra* can and must be used to transform the planet.

In the deepest sense, this vision of evolutionary sexuality is a gift to us from the Divine Mother. She wants to redeem our bodies, redeem our sense of our bodies, show us that she lives just as much in our bodies and in our genitals as in the skies, and mountains, and mystical revelations. She wants us to experience in the core of life her great bliss fire; but She doesn't want us to experience it simply to feel glorious and empowered. She wants us to feel glorious and empowered so that we can be Her tireless agents of transfiguration in reality.

What I envisage is a whole army of lovers coming together to bring in a reign of compassion and justice fueled by this sublime, liberated sexual energy. There are two images that I think of. One is of Jesus and Mary Magdalene. When I contemplate that relationship at the deepest level, I feel that Mary Magdalene, by mirroring Jesus, by loving him, by worshiping him, by pouring herself out to him, filled him with sacred feminine energy for his great mission.

The second image is a gay image because I'm a gay teacher—it's of the Spartan warriors at Thermopylae. The Spartans' special forces were homosexual lovers. Just before they went into the battle in which they lost their lives but prevented the Persians from invading Greece, they bathed, they adorned each other, and they made love so that they would find the fearless courage to do what their heroism called them to do—prevent, at any cost, the Persian invasion of Greece. Without the sacrifice that flamed out from their noble passion for each other and from this celebration of each other's inner and outer beauty, we would not have the Parthenon or the Greek vision of democracy that continues to inspire our world.

One transmission from my own past is, to me, the key for this transformed evolutionary sexuality. It was given to me by my most beloved teacher, the great Christian mystic, Father Bede Griffiths. In a way it's strange that it was given to me by him because he was, at the time, eighty-six years old and a celibate. But he knew a thing or two, Father Bede, and he had the deepest and wisest and most all-embracing wisdom. He also had a comprehensive knowledge from first-hand experience of the birth of the Divine in matter because he was living that transfiguration process. He was a sign of the great birth.

One day, we were sitting under a tree at his ashram in southern India and very excitedly he turned to me and said, "Andrew, Andrew, Andrew, I've got it about sex. I really have." He was fascinated about sex because he understood that sexual energy was potentially divine energy.

He said, "Look, you cannot deny sexuality, because I've been to so many ashrams and monasteries and they're full of lunatics who have repressed themselves. And you can't just simply express it, because I've met all sorts of people who have come to me in sessions who've done things I can't spell, didn't know existed, and who seemed extremely unhappy. It's neither suppression nor promiscuity."

Then Bede's face broke into a radiant smile. "What you need to do with sexual energy is to consecrate it, to really devote it, at its essence and at its root and in its expression and in its goal, to the full vision of the Divine in transcendent reality and in immanent reality. If you do that, then your sexuality becomes a form of worship that initiates you into the essence of the Universe and into the dream of God to establish the kingdom on Earth."

The Sacred and Epic Aspects of Evolutionary Sexuality
—A Dialogue between Chris Saade and Andrew Harvey

Chris Saade: The image of consecrating our sexual energy for the glory of the dream of the Divine, of love, justice, and peace is very powerful. I was fortunate enough to have a teacher in my twenties who told me a simple but powerful concept about sexuality. The core of his message was that when you are involved in making love with your partner, always remember the soul of the one you are making love with and always what the act of love symbolizes. In the epic traditions, physical lovemaking was an honoring of the Divine in and through our partner. It was also a sacred recalling of the primal energies that created the Universe and are now creating the dream of love of the Divine on Earth.

When we reclaim the profound meaning of sexuality, sexuality reveals its magnificence. Unfortunately, with the isolation of relationships from their connection to the larger web of life, sexuality also becomes privatized and diminished. Sexuality becomes a routine and trivialized act that is merely a good release, or helpful with stress. It loses its richness. It becomes an act that is reduced in its meaning. It loses its symbolic richness. In the epic traditions, it is said that when two lovers get together and abandon themselves to loving each other, the God and the Goddess come and love each other through them. The two lovers become a temple for the Divine to express love. The Divine is always involved in bringing love into the world, so through the beautiful act of lovemaking, we gather the energies of love so we can become greater servants of the vision of love in the world.

When we look at evolutionary sexuality, we create a space for lovemaking that is sacred and we offer it up to the Divine for the good of the world. The space of lovemaking needs to be protected from any psychological issues that the relationship is having. These problems will continue, of course, and will have to be resolved. However, we keep any psychological stress outside the door because when we come to the love bed, we enter a temple. By disrobing, we temporarily remove all of the unfinished business and disappointments, and we offer our lovemaking as a prayer to the Divine—as an honoring of the beauty of life, in our partner, in the Earth, and in the world. We offer ourselves as a prayer for the continuation of creation and the expansion of the idea of love, for the coming of the day of jubilee and greater peace on Earth.

Andrew Harvey: I love what you're saying, Chris, because the essence of evolutionary sexuality is that through it, we become a conduit of the ecstatic bliss energies of the Father/Mother.

Chris Saade: Exactly.

Andrew Harvey: In experiencing these energies, we experience the depth of our own human divinity. We are also invested with the power we then need to dedicate our sacred evolutionary purpose in the Universe!

Chris Saade: Definitely. Definitely.

Andrew Harvey: What is so wonderful about the ancient Indian tradition, the Hindu Shiva tradition, of which I am a particular devotee, is that it understands this at the most exquisite and profound level. There's a poem I love by Jnaneshwar, "The Nectar of Self Awareness." Jnaneshwar lived in the thirteenth century and died at twenty-one, having revolutionized Indian mysticism. In this poem he says, "I celebrate the God and the Goddess. The lover out of boundless love has taken the form of the Beloved." Then he writes, "The lover swallows up the beloved, and then separates for the joy of being two."

Chris Saade: Yes.

Andrew Harvey: In the tantric act of sexual celebration, we experience the two aspects of the Father/Mother. We experience their union and their fusion in total ecstasy, and we also experience the separation in deep union, so that the Absolute in us can contemplate the relative and know that the relative is a face of the Absolute, streaming the Absolute's love towards us.

Chris Saade: It is that moment of surrendering to a total union and knowing we will emerge again with our separate individuality once again. We individuals, stronger and enriched, are once again authentic, unique individuals and, as such, continue our co-creative dance. We return to that question from the epic tradition, "What is love?" Love is the moment in which we affirm life over the forces of destruction.

Then the next question was: "Who are we loving?" We are loving the Divine expressed in the authentic spirit and the authentic embodiment of our partner. We realize within that sacred moment of physical union that the tenderness we bring to our partner—the tender caresses, touches, melting into their smell, basking in their energy—is a tenderness we are offering to the Divine that is alive in the spirit and body of our partner. This shifts everything, because we realize that what we are loving is the force of love in the other person. It is the same presence of love that is working to transform the world. The tenderness of our touch becomes a prayer to the Divine—to love itself.

Again, romancing our partner with words, sexual touch, and poetic statements is romancing the Divine within them. In the love chamber, our souls—be it in a homosexual or heterosexual relationship—carry the

Divine in the dance that holds up the world for love, compassion, and justice. Lovemaking is a great ritual of beauty and meaning.

We are romancing nothing less than the Goddess or the God within our beloved partner. Therefore, what is asked of us is nothing less than total abandon, passion, and giving of ourselves in that sacred moment. As we hold sexuality from a sacred perspective, sexuality reveals itself as a celebratory and mythic moment, separate from the psychological bargaining we impose on it. The sexual dance becomes freed from the drain of linking it to our moods and demands. It becomes a moment of ritual, where the more we give and receive, the more we allow the generative forces of life to flow through us and to empower us for love and for meaningful service.

Escaping Privatization and Sacred Illustrations of Evolutionary Sexuality
—A Dialogue between Andrew Harvey and Chris Saade

Andrew Harvey: I'd love to dance with the themes that you've been talking about by telling two stories. The first is a heterosexual story and the second is a homosexual story. It's actually a vision that I myself had which began to liberate me.

The first story takes place in Khajuraho, a site in northern India where the greatest erotic temples of India are all clustered together on a magnificent five acres. In these erotic temples are some of the most beautiful sculptures of the world. You see celebrated all possible erotic combinations, but they are not pornographic. Each of these sculptures is a representation of the embodied divine bliss that can be experienced when lovers abandon themselves to the truth of the primordial

195

divine origin of sexuality.

I was taking a group of rather shocked, slightly puritanical, Americans, who had never seen anything like this, around Khajuraho. We had the most wonderful, soft-voiced, priestly guide. After we had gone around the temples and registered some of the shocked reactions, he and I were walking in the gardens and he said to me, "I wish I could've told them the truth." I asked, "What is the truth?" He looked at me and said, "When I love the yoni of my wife, I am loving the vast darkness out of which the whole Universe is created. And when she worships my phallus, she is worshiping Shiva's phallus that is the seminal power behind the creation of the Universe."

That was an amazing instruction for me. It wasn't just what he said, it was how he said it. I knew that I was in the presence of somebody who truly understood and lived and embodied the *Tantra,* because everything about him was suffused with this golden glow of gratitude and reverence and intimate celebration of life.

The second story is really about how I came as a gay man to a similar revelation. It was hard won because in the traditional tantric systems, it is usually said that tantra can only flower between men and women. In some of the patriarchal tantric systems, the men have the primordial place and the woman is just there to raise the divine energy of the masculine, which is, of course, outrageous and abusive.

I was deeply studying these traditions and staying in Mahabalipuram, a charming, funky, broken-down fishing village. It is home to some of the greatest ancient temples and statues in southern India, with alchemical representations in stone of the divine world of the future, the world that we are trying to build now.

I had a dream while I was there. In this dream I was in the Shore Temple, one of the most exquisite temples in India, small but very holy, and beautifully located by the Bay of Bengal. In the dream, I was in the Shore temple late at night alone. Shiva as a young man suddenly entered. He was naked from the waist up with a lungi of gold silk tied around his waist, blindingly beautiful. Standing in front of me, with a full erection, flinging aside his lungi, he said, "Do with me what you want. Love me and worship me." The electric bliss that flooded me as I obeyed him permanently altered my vision of sexuality and relationships. It also permanently convinced me that homosexual love, lived at this highest level, is as blessed and powerful a vehicle of evolutionary love as heterosexual passion.

This vision whose power never leaves me liberated me to worship and be worshiped and to know that my deepest sexual impulses were not blasphemous or any way limiting on my path to liberation. It liberated me also to know that if they could be dedicated to this worship of the Divine Beloved in the other, the Shiva in my male partner, and if I could worship that Shiva as *Shiva Ardhanarishvara,* the Shiva that is half masculine and half feminine, then a huge flowering of sacred energy for and in us both would take place. In my forties and fifties, I was blessed to live this revelation with my husband and another tantric partner.

Chris Saade: When we understand that the sexual act contains so much of the Divine and so much worship within it—then we come to comprehend the meaning of evolutionary sexuality. One of the problems that most people face when sexuality is privatized and deprived of its mythic dimension, is that sexuality becomes caught in judgment and shame. If sex is not a mystical participation in the greater energy of love, then a myriad of psychological issues arise: "What do I think about my body? What's happening to your body? What do you think about me? Do you like me enough? Are you doing it correctly? Am I good enough?" et cetera... All these issues paralyze the sexual act, or at a minimum drain a lot of the energy out of it. In sexuality that is isolated and trivialized, it can feel alive for the initial novelty of the other person, but after a while it starts dying. It becomes a repetitive act.

It does make a great difference when we see sex the way you, Andrew, and ancients are talking about it, i.e. that by making love to our partner we are inviting the Goddess or God in them to come and dance fully with us. We are affirming the authenticity of our partner, in spirit and body, as sacred. We are inviting the cosmic energy of love to emerge from the sexual encounter. Sexual love becomes a source of energy and a source of freedom because it is not only about two people. It becomes an act of ecstatic celebration of the energies transforming the world through love and for love.

Then the sexual encounter becomes something that is far beyond what is happening to our bodies. Sex becomes two people joining in co-creating a ritual to affirm life against everything that is trying to crush down. It is a place where a couple can discover the passionate energy that they can then take with them out into the world. The feminine is affirmed, the masculine is affirmed, the heterosexual is affirmed, and the homosexual is affirmed—all in the sanctity and truth of being a reflection of Divine love itself.

But through this beautiful process we cannot forget our brokenness. We have to respectfully include our wounds. Our beauty exists in light and in brokenness. In the act of love, like everywhere else, reality has to be welcomed. We bring our brokenness to our sexuality and our lover becomes the one who holds, respects and makes love to our brokenness, grief, vulnerabilities, and trembling, as well as our strengths. Everything is brought into this picture and we are back to the question, "Who are we making love to and what does it mean to make love?" We are making love to the sacred in the authentic uniqueness of our partner.

It is so important to stay conscious of the incredible beauty and greatness that is present within the moment when two people embrace each other in spirit and bodies. It is a moment that is truly eternal. It has no beginning and no end and it reaches far beyond the temporal space of lovemaking. Lovers who have this experience and come together in ecstatic orgasm have similar responses: "We've gone beyond time and space. I feel like I've known you forever. I feel like I'm going to be with you forever. I experience so much power and energy after I have been in your arms…" Unleashing the energy of the soul, body, mind, and heart of our partner is a gift from the Divine. By holding the presence of our partner tenderly, and bringing their heart and body close to our own body and heart, we experience in the here and now the eternal forces working to bring the day of jubilee, transformation, and peace.

What a gift it is! But we must always remember that we are loving the full being of the other, and must learn to be sexually and tenderly romantic with their brokenness, beauty, and trembling, as they would be with ours. It is about celebrating the full Divine—the blissful and grieving aspects of the heart of the Divine. It is all the same thing, reflecting itself everywhere and within the love bed where we love the full authentic reality of our partner.

Sacred Sexuality as the Co-Creation of Universal Loving Energy
—A Dialogue between Chris Saade and Andrew Harvey

Andrew Harvey: I have had several great tantric teachers and I've never spoken their names and I have never given the full instruction that they gave me because traditionally in India, tantric instructions are passed verbally and secretly. They are not given to people who haven't achieved a certain level of maturity, because when you are dealing with this primordial energy, any misuse of it will explode in your face. But an old woman in Benares gave me this four-point ritual for blissful tantric initiation, that I now want to share with all those who aspire to the evolutionary tantra we are celebrating.

One. Always begin your lovemaking with your tantric partner by invoking the full glory and full presence of the Father/Mother in whatever way you want. She had several mantras because of her Indian tradition, but what I suggest is that before you make love, ask the Divine to come down into your lovemaking, possess your bodies, illumine your hearts, and instruct you that the bliss that you experience is the *ananda* that is creating the Universe. Ask the Divine to open every cell to the downpour of the golden bliss energy of the Father/Mother.

Two. Leave the problems of your psychological involvement with your partner outside the bedroom door. Say together a deep prayer of protection. Imagine your love bed surrounded by rings of purifying flame so that no negative energies of sex hatred or body hatred or trauma or shadow or anger or need to control or anything from the external forces that don't want you to experience your divinity, none of them can get through those flames.

Three. Give yourself absolutely and shamelessly to the other as an offering, as a prayer, as a worshiper. These three are all holy, but what blew my brains out was when she told me about the fourth stage.

Four. My wild old teacher told me that one of the things that most saddened her is the way in which people waste the sacred power of orgasm. Orgasm is potentially the moment not only of the making of a child, which is amazing enough, but on the divine level, the power of a tantric orgasm shared by two people who are worshiping each other is a power that can and must and should be dedicated to the bringing about of the Divine on Earth. Her instruction: At the moment when the bliss culminates in an explosion of energy, dedicate that energy to all the four directions, to all sentient beings, to the liberation of justice, and compassion on every level in the world. Then rest together knowing that through these four stages you have made an act of worship for the establishment of the Divine in matter on the Earth in every institution, in every art, in every science. That is the way the act of lovemaking becomes both an act of private divinization and an act that contributes to the flooding of the whole Earth with the blissful love energies of God that inspire sacred action.

Chris Saade: We are co-creating an energetic field that helps the collective consciousness move in the direction of love. Lovemaking becomes an ecstatic prayer that two people do together in the co-creative dance with each other and with the Divine. We discover our unique authenticity through love—the generosity of love. As we discover our authentic path, we start receiving guidance, blessing, vision, and inspiration. But we must be willing to give ourselves to the dream of love in order for this to happen. Love, authenticity, and solidarity with the Earth and others, as well as blessings we receive, are all part of the same luminous web.

When we come to sexuality, it is the same principle. It is an offering of our authentic self in love and through love. It is a total dedication to pleasuring and nurturing the other physically and emotionally. It is not a negotiation in which, "I'll do that for you if you do that for me, and how about this or that." This turns our sexual experience into a banal act that becomes subject to discussion and haggling. Lovemaking is, I believe, meant to be an act of abundant generosity—where we focus upon the pleasuring and nurturing of this wonderful being, our partner, who is carrying within them the heroic spirit of love. By this total offering, we free ourselves from restraints and from shame. We are in an act of giving, loving, and realizing that our partner needs and deserves reaffirmation of their intrinsic beauty through our touch, kisses, and love. It is through these intentional actions of love and generosity that the authenticity of their being is mirrored back in its beauty and dignity.

We come to realize that there is a lover within us that is beyond what we ever dreamed possible. Something primal is unleashed within us that is connected to the energy of the Divine. From this, we see as two people want to fully please and give themselves to the other, we become fuller and more realized. There is a creation, a co-creation much bigger than we are, that overtakes us and delivers us to a place where our deep heart energies are nurtured. In this place of generosity and abandon to the forces of love, we are optimal. We are our authentic selves, as are our partners, fitting seamlessly with one another. But for this to happen it is vitally important to free ourselves from the idea that sexuality is just a biological urge, or just a mundane act.

Andrew Harvey: It's an archetypal birth!

Chris Saade: An archetypal birth and an incredible story. There is so much in it.

Andrew Harvey: The Big Bang is the orgasm of the Father/Mother. When you have a sacred orgasm you're re-experiencing that Big Bang, and you're adding to the evolutionary power that began the Universe.

Something intrigues me very much: How do we bring brokenness into the relationship? Chris, you gave a beautiful illustration when you said to cradle the vulnerability of the other. I want to make this discussion about brokenness a little deeper and more edgy because one of the things that has to happen in evolutionary sexuality is a fearless embrace of the shadow side of sexuality. Not a repression of it, but a welcoming of it into consciousness and using what could be a dark, perverse power to actually fuel the ecstasy that leads to the birthing big bang of truth. This is a difficult act because it means facing the dark sides of your own sexuality without shame and without judgment.

If you are able, with the full consent of your partner, to bring your fantasies into play in the depth of this sacred abandon to each other, then you'll find that the lovemaking you're then able to enjoy will be fiercer, wilder, more impassioned and even more completely healing.

Chris Saade: You come to understand that the fantasy and the erotic imagination of yourself and your partner are the healthy imagination of life itself. It is not that you are dissatisfied with your partner; it is that life is so rich with sexual imagery. All that energy can be used to enhance the sexual intimacy of the couple. For again, the world lives in our sexuality—not just the couple. Individuals are never separate from the world. The more authentic we are, the more we uncover layers of ourselves that are of the world, of the ancestors, and of the Earth. Love (and fidelity) channels the larger imagination into blessing the couple.

Andrew Harvey: Erotic wildness.

Chris Saade: Yes—erotic wildness, sexual symbolisms, and aspects of the world that arouse our sexual energy. These things remind us of the intimate dance of the sacred bodies that we are. We need to realize, and celebrate from an evolutionary perspective, the fact that our partner carries within them the whole world and the whole Universe. Our partner carries within them the imagination of all people who lived before them, of tribal sexuality, and the imagination of the future as well. What Andrew is saying, which is so important, is, "Do I use that imagination in a way that is destructive or banal?"

Andrew Harvey: Or private or shameful or weird or something I keep for myself? Or do I pour it into the relationship itself?

Chris Saade: Do I offer all of my being as a way to empower love and enrich the relationship? This means a deep and fearless respect between two people. In a privatized relationship we think, "This is *our* relationship, *our* sexuality, *our* bodies—so why would there be any other imagination?"

From an evolutionary perspective we know that we, as individuals, carry the world within us. We carry the past, present, and future. We carry the Earth and the Universe. We carry the prayers, imagination, and the hopes of millions. Once we understand this and respect it in one another, then we can bring it together as an offering into this space of fidelity and commitment to fan the fires of love and Eros. The purpose of sexuality is to keep us alive, strong, and regenerated for the great work. Our role through lovemaking is to fill the heart and body with an ample infusion of love's energy.

Andrew Harvey: In classical tantric terms this is very profound. These ancient systems knew the whole story in so many ways. My teacher in Benares told me that if a man is truly worshiping his wife or his woman as the Goddess, he's worshiping not just one face of the Goddess, he's worshiping all the different aspects of the Goddess in one woman. This is how he can bring his love of all different kinds of women, his love for the Lakshmi women, his love for the Durga women, his love for the Shakti women, his love for the prostitute women, his love for the married women, his love for all the different faces of the Goddess. He can pour all of them into her and bring all of them into his worship of her.

If, as a gay man, I'm worshiping my lover as Shiva, Shiva has a thousand faces: he's a warrior, he's a king, he's a lover, he's a yogi, he's a hermit, he's a mad man, and he's a punk. I can put my love for all of these different facets of the sacred male into my worship of the man who is my Shiva.

Chris Saade: By loving my beloved, I am also loving the world within her—the world on Earth and the world in Heaven. This is where commitment becomes very important, because this commitment allows people to create a space where these worlds can unfold and be realized. I would realize that I am passionately here for her and she for me, and that together we are going to let that energy come through us. We fully understand that sexual energy does not belong to us. We cannot privatize sexual energy. It is a cosmic energy that is flowing through everything—through animals, plants, rocks, and so on. The big question always remains the same: how can we be strong as individuals with a sharp individuality and at the same time remain aware of the intimate union that ties us to the greater web of life? Eros is both a very powerful individual force as well as a collective energy that binds us to all of life.

Andrew Harvey: And glittering in the sun on rivers, everything is Eros.

Chris Saade: Exactly, Eros is everywhere and if we do not treat it as sacred, then it will be utilized for destructive purposes, and even abuse. You can perceive the degradation of Eros when you see the sexual exploitation of women and young children through the sex slave trade. It is our responsibility as evolutionary couples to acknowledge the power of this energy and channel it for love and meaningful creativity.

Our work is to use that cosmic energy, let it move through us, and allow it to transform us. We cannot avoid it, and any attempts to deny its powerful presence would mean that we invite it to be used by destructive and commercialized forces. By doing this, we also deprive ourselves of that which allows us to feel the strength, bliss, and joy that enables us to stand up successfully to oppressive and life-denying forces. Authenticity is true power—authenticity in service of love.

Confronting the Resistances to Evolutionary Sexuality
—A Dialogue between Andrew Harvey and Chris Saade

Andrew Harvey: Now it's time to confront all the resistances in us to this evolutionary sexuality. The first resistance is that we all inherit a brutal legacy of body hatred and body shame. Experiencing your body, and the body of other beings, as truly holy temples takes an immense amount of inner work. And it's continuing work. For all the years of tantric practice that I have done, and all the years I begged the Mother to reveal my body to myself as a holy temple—the holiest of temples—I find that I still have body shame and body hatred that I constantly need to work on and make conscious and offer up to healing by her grace.

Chris Saade: This is very important. It is crucial to recapture the beauty of each and everyone's body. Every physical manifestation, whatever it may be, can be gorgeous and beautiful. What commercialism has done is indoctrinated the masses that only a selection of figures of the human body are to be desired and worshipped, while all others are to be reviled. To refuse acceptance of this authoritarian abuse of body image, and to rebel against this indoctrination, is to realize and understand that every physical manifestation of the human body is worthy of being loved and revered with total abandon and total passion. Our authenticity will reveal to us our own physical chemistry with others, but that is the freedom of subjectivity, not a norm to be imposed on others. The mind has to refuse the shaming of any physical type. Sexuality, like life, thrives in the respect for diversity. Sexuality is a spiritual experience—a spiritual path that joins Earth and Heaven together.

Andrew Harvey: Absolutely. We have to face, though, that authentic Tantric sexuality endangers the ego. Because if you do go into those realms of ecstatic bliss, you don't know where you begin and where the other ends. We all say that we long to experience this. But there are many people who get terrified when they experience this blissful oneness, because they no longer have control. If you're going to really experience this evolutionary sex field, you're going to have to lose control. Really lose control.

The resistance comes if you haven't trained in your own private spiritual practice, and in your own relationship to your body, to create a vessel strong enough to contain the vast energies of authentic evolutionary love. If you haven't created stability—through exercise, through diet, through the honoring of your body, through prayer and deep understanding of the mystical inter-penetration of transcendence and immanence— then the energies that come in can create illness and psychological craziness and arouse wild unexpected sides of the shadow, which will erupt and hijack you. You are, in fact, "riding a tiger," as the tantric mystics say, and unless you are strong, supple, and balanced enough to ride that tiger, you'll tumble off and get eaten.

Chris Saade: An energy from the heart of the Universe has been gifted to us, and we have to create a space for it, attend to it, respect it, and get ourselves ready for it. A practice that helps a couple come to that sacred space with open hearts is to take the time to sit together and honor one another's spirit before making love. Honoring touches the heart, awakens the body, and when appropriate, calls forth the erotic energies. This is an invitation for the spirit to fully enter into the lovemaking experience.

The second part of this practice is to offer your lovemaking as a prayer for the world. Ask the Divine to fill you with the energy to be able to love and adore one another and then promise to offer that energy in service of the world—of those deprived of their rights, of children that have been abandoned... Sexual love as a dedication and offering of powerful life energies!

Third, take the time and tell your partner how unbelievably beautiful he or she is. How every part of their body, regardless of appearance (no ifs, ands, or buts), is a miraculous manifestation of the beauty of the Divine.

How it is a privilege to love them physically. Take time to say this to each other, because when you do so you are invoking the sacred to be present.

We need to hear this. We are living in a world that sexualizes everything and then devalues sexuality down to being a mere physical release. We need to hear, again and again, from our partner how sacred the connection is, how sacred the relationship is. And when we speak, we need to hear it ourselves, so that it becomes increasingly more present for us. It is a great gift that we are given, to be able to love each other from the heart through the body. It's a miracle. We cannot take the amazement of physical love for granted.

Andrew Harvey: It's the secret of embodiment. It's the secret of the incarnation, which is why body hatred has continually aborted the birth of the Divine in matter and why evolutionary love needs to reclaim a divine and consecrated sexuality in this way.

Chapter 10
Pursuing Evolutionary Love

Envision a World of Engaged Evolutionary Relationships
—A Dialogue between Andrew Harvey and Chris Saade

Andrew Harvey: We're nearing the end of our epic conversation together. Now I would love you to take a deep breath and describe your vision of what realized evolutionary love could make available to the world. What would a world of increasingly divinized, embodied couples actually look like? What would they enshrine and achieve?

Chris Saade: We know that the transformation of the world toward love's vision, the expansion of democratic freedoms, peace, and justice is going to come from the minority, not the majority. It's going to come from a very dedicated soulful minority—like Mother Teresa, Gandhi, Nelson Mandela, Florence Nightingale, Martin Luther King Jr. and the people who were with him—who have known the authenticity of the unique self that

215

they were, mined its unique power, and felt rivers of love flowing within themselves. Not that it was done perfectly—of course their passion was manifested with mistakes and with brokenness—but they have known the power of the freedom of authenticity and the great generosity of love. More people are arising with the confidence of epic lovers who are speaking vigorously, though imperfectly, both the freedom of individual authenticity as well as a vision of love and solidarity for the world and the Earth.

Now what we are seeing, are people who are doing this evolutionary dance as a couple and within relationships. Uniting the creative forces emerging from the heart within a couple does not just double the power, it exponentially multiplies that power. A quantum leap of heart and mind erupts. A healthy relationship that harbors the freedom of authenticity and the passion of love, when it is dedicated to a common vision of social transformation and liberation, unleashes energies bigger than anything we have seen so far. As you have said, Andrew, most people working for peace and justice in the world might feel isolated. Couples doing this work co-creatively, and then hopefully in community, are moving away from the paradigm of the lone creator. The partnership of a couple enamored by a larger vision of authenticity, democratic freedoms, peace, and justice unleashes possibilities of strength and compassion beyond our imagination.

What we would see are couples that are able to go beyond criticizing and psychoanalyzing each other's behavior. They would recognize the beauty and the strength of each other's authenticity: authenticity of personality, mind, psyche, heart, and aspirations. What would become central is not the endless arguments about who is correct and who is not, who is more functional, who has the best analysis and perception, but rather the profound respect of the freedom to be who one is, and to affirm one's given nature. What we would see are individuals committed to honoring each other's personality (with its particularities, lacks, and gifts) and a deep appreciation of unique and authentic idiosyncrasies. We would see individuals who desire to intentionally create, through their freedom of authenticity, a space where the energies of love can abound, and where freedom and love are deepened and enhanced by partners serving together humanity and the Earth. Criticizing each other's behavior and psychoanalyzing the roots of desires and aspirations, divides the couple even further. It weakens, if not deadens their love. The affirmation of the freedom of each other's inalienable authenticity of self, as well as the affirmation of the passion to serve love's vision in the world, strengthens the bond of a couple and regenerates its intensity. Authenticity, love, and social solidarity become an ever-progressing and mutually deepening spiral. Authenticity is crucial for a thriving love in a relationship, as is social solidarity.

Andrew Harvey: I would like to add, before we end, that this vision of evolutionary love could potentially heal the tragic split between men and women that we're witnessing at this moment. Men have never felt more disempowered, more bewildered. They don't know what sacred masculinity is because all the old paradigms of it are being rubbled and there is so much relentless focus on how the masculine has oppressed the feminine. Many women are now quite rightly very angry at what has happened. Women are also going through a crisis of identity because they're finding it hard to integrate the different sides of the feminine, especially the grand ferocity of the dark feminine, so demonized by patriarchy, let alone their own inherent masculine. There is tremendous disarray, mutual suspicion, and suffering going on today in heterosexual relationships.

In evolutionary love, we're trying to bring a new vision for heterosexual couples to aspire to in which the man will feel worshipped as the Shiva he is and the woman will feel worshipped as the Goddess she is. The psychological wrangling will have a chance of easing and ceasing and the baptism and initiation into divine archetypal life can become the source of immense healing.

I'd also like to say something about homosexual relationships. In my experience, the homosexual world is still a ravaged by internalized homophobia, and rejection of the body, even as it is falsely promoting and celebrating it in strange and self-destructive ways. I invite all my gay brothers and sisters to realize that through the celebration of their divine sexuality and the dedication of the joy and energy they uncover through it to sacred action, they too can play their sacred and unique part in the creation of a new world.

Chris Saade: That is so beautiful, Andrew. May we continue to affirm the beauty of love in its different forms of manifestation: romantic, friendship, social, heterosexual, gay...I now want to ask you something as we close. You speak about the ways in which people who have a passion for the world and a passion for peace and justice many times find themselves alone because others might be afraid or overwhelmed by their passion. What do you tell people about this issue? Can we be passionate about transformation in the world and be fully invested in building a relationship?

Andrew Harvey: Yes! Absolutely! If you ground both in a total adoration and surrender to the Divine. The Divine is the only force strong enough to fuel both the kind of rigor and power and efficiency and truth and passion and energy that you need for your work in the world, and the energy and passion and peace and rigor and power that you're going to need for your relationship. Only the Divine can do it.

Final Recommendations and Encouragements
—from Chris Saade and Andrew Harvey

Chris Saade: I would like to end this conversation with some recommendations:

- Do *not* be afraid of the welling up in your heart of the great passion for freedom, justice, peace, and inclusion! Do not shy away from that incredible pull that you feel to serve the full dream of love. There are great forces of love awakening our hearts. Trust that passion! It will lead you where you need to go.

- Authenticity and authenticity! Unfold and develop the rich fabric of your authentic nature. Honor and develop the unique self that you are. Honor and support the unique self of your partner.

- Support the passion of your partner for transformation in the world. Become the greatest support for their attempt to affect change in the world, and invite them to support your passion. Doing this for each other will expand love and Eros in the relationship, and allow you to bring to fruition the project you seek to co-create in service to the world.

- Practice perceiving your partner through the lenses of authenticity. Rather than seeing defects and psychoanalyzing them, uphold the authentic traits of your partner. Their lacks are inherently related to their gifts. Lacks are the empty space through which authentic gifts emerge. Fully enjoy their gifts, and accept and honor their lacks as part and parcel of the gifts. You also have lacks, and they are part of the exquisite beauty of your being. Vulnerability is the precondition of ecstasy.

- And for those of you who are not for the time being in a committed relationship, look for a man or a woman who affirms and respects their own authenticity, and who is passionate about their journey for peace and justice. Such a person will be much more prone to give and receive love. Love emerges from a sturdy sense of authenticity and a deep care for humanity and the Earth. Do not sell out the largeness of your heart. Seek partners and relationships with those who are committed to that journey. When you do find that potential partner who is compatible to you in these imperative ways, be daring in your love and extremely generous in the offering of yourself. Such a soul relationship will not be perfect, but it will have the fire of intimacy, the communion of hearts, as well as the soothing waters of tenderness.

- Finally, do not lose heart because of the difficulties, setbacks, or disappointments on the journey toward evolutionary love. The journey of evolutionary love is demanding. We are growing into it. We are not yet there, but are moving toward it. Evolutionary relationships are a gorgeous and amazing tapestry we are beginning to weave. It is worth all the effort and the difficulties. Strivings in that direction will deepen love. Love is the ultimate ecstasy—loving who we are: our personality and our body, as well as loving our beloved, our family of choice, the noble souls of heart, the Earth, the children of our planet, the aspirations of humanity, the animal world… and of course the Divine Source as we understand it.

Andrew Harvey: Let me end by saying how grateful I am, Chris, to share this vision and journey with you, and how much I have learned from our dance together. I want to finish with two more quotations that I cherish and celebrate from *The Radiance Sutras*, and follow them with a glorious Sufi prayer written by Sheikh Ansari, one of Islam's greatest mystics:

> *Join with the Goddess and God*
> *Who are making love*
> *In every particle of creation …*
>
> *And with every breath*
> *Bless the life that surround you.*

* * * * * *

The light of consciousness illumines the world
The world reflects this splendor.
Energy and matter, essence and manifestation
Reveal each other to each other.

Individual soul and cosmic energy
Pulsing heart and infinite awareness—
Are secret lovers, always merging in oneness.
When the secret slips out, there is laughter
And a flash of brilliance in the air.

And now for the prayer. I say at moments through my day and invite all evolutionary adventurers to say it too with profound devotion:

O Beloved, give me a heart
I can pour out in thanksgiving.
Give me life
So I can spend it
Working for the salvation of the world.

About the Authors

Andrew Harvey is an internationally acclaimed poet, novelist, translator, mystical scholar, and spiritual teacher. He has written and edited more than 30 books—including the best-selling titles *The Hope* and *The Tibetan Book of Living and Dying*. He has won the Christmas Humphries Prize (*A Journey in Ladakh*), the Nautilus Prize twice (*The Hope*, *Light the Flame*), and appeared in two recent films (*Dancing in the Flames*, and Ethan Hawke's *Seymour: An Introduction*). He was also the subject of the 1993 BBC film documentary *The Making of a Modern Mystic*. He has taught at Oxford University, Cornell University, Hobart and William Smith Colleges, The California Institute of Integral Studies, and the University of Creation Spirituality as well as at various spiritual centers throughout the United States. He is the founder and director of the Institute of Sacred Activism. He is a kind-hearted rascal with a penchant for red pashminas, Maria Callas, white lions and Chicago pizza.

Chris Saade is an author, life coach, psychological and philosophical teacher, and the co-director of the Olive Branch Center with his wife Jessie Thompson. After closing his psychotherapy private practice, Saade spent 20 years training therapists, coaches, and ministers in his two models: *Integra: 6 Keys for Heart-Centered Living*, and *Individual Authenticity and Global Solidarity*.

Saade has led nearly 250 multi-day cutting-edge workshops for professionals and the general public. He continues to offer personal life-coaching.

Born in Beirut, Lebanon, he was involved in peace groups before and during the Lebanese war. Those difficult years lead him to develop a great respect for freedom, authenticity, diversity, peace, and a passion for justice, especially for children.

Saade is the author of *Second Wave Spirituality: Passion for Peace, Passion for Justice*; and *Prayers for Peace and Justice*; as well as *Prayers from the Heart*. The Saade-Harvey team has also created the CD set: *Sacred Activism and the Epic Spirituality of Love*. He resides in San Diego.

© Permission to use image here and on back cover granted by Ginger Wagoner, Photosynthesis Inc.